## Praise for *Communicate to Influence*

Maybe the most undervalued, but critically important, aspect of leadership is the ability to connect with others. The Decker approach to communication offers the framework for becoming far more than a first-class communicator; it offers the framework to become a first-class connector. If you want to grow your leadership skills in a manner that is authentic and lasting, there is no better place to start than with Decker Communications.

—Walt Bettinger, President and CEO of The Charles Schwab Company

A breakthrough book for those who have to persuade—and that's all of us. The Communicator's Roadmap will move you from influence to inspire.

—Chip Conley, Founder of Joie de Vivre Hotels
and bestselling author of *Emotional Equations*

Effective communication is the #1 skill needed in business today, and the Deckers have unlocked the key ingredient: communicating to inspire an audience. I sent my entire leadership team through their course, and we have achieved incredible results in a very short time. Inspirational communication—and the culture it helped create—led my team to achieve what many thought impossible. What an invaluable skill set! This book is a must-read.

—Jennifer Van Buskirk, President of Cricket Wireless

The Deckers' practical approach will help every businessperson build the critical skill of communicating in a way that influences action. I've been using and loving their method for years—it's great to see their powerful ideas in this must-read that really hits the mark!

—Jim Lecinski, VP of Americas Customer Solutions at Google

Communicating with and inspiring people is at the core of all we do. First I, and then our company, learned how to truly communicate and inspire clients and customers by following the methodologies in this book. Ben and Kelly have not only developed a proven roadmap to successful communication, they have taken the journey with us. Great communication is critical in all roles, and when you get it right, it is beautiful to watch. This book will help you get it right.

—John Esposito, President of Stoli Group USA
(and former President and CEO of Bacardi and Moët Hennessy)

Ben and Kelly's approach gives people the courage to change, tapping into intrinsic motivators, which ultimately drive behavior.

—John Thiel, Head of Merrill Lynch Wealth Management

Leaders at every business big and small can be more effective once they learn to Communicate to Influence. I've seen the results myself, professionally and personally.

—Robert Kyncl, Head of Content and Business Operations at YouTube

Applying the Decker Method changed not only how I give presentations and speeches, it transformed the communication strategy for our entire organization. *Communicate to Influence* is a must-read for leaders who truly want to make a difference both on the stage and off.

—Ernie Sadau, CEO of Christus Health

Learning how to Communicate to Influence helped me loosen up, connect with my team, and actually create the change I wanted. When I prepare using the Decker Method, I confidently communicate critical messages to key business influencers.

—Janet Risi, CEO of IPC, SUBWAY® Purchasing Cooperative

My favorite part of this book is that the Deckers drill some famous people: Obama, Mayer, Zuckerberg. Nothing is more amusing or informative than learning how the emperors have no clothes. I hope they never write about me.

—Guy Kawasaki, Chief Evangelist of Canva
and bestselling author of *The Art of the Start, version 2.0*

The most powerful aspect of using the Decker Method is that it allows you to organize your thoughts and present them in a way that connects you with your audience. Since taking the Decker course 11 years ago, I have never spoken publicly without using it—and never plan to. The method teaches you how to personalize even the most difficult message.

What I enjoy about it the most is that it allows me to be myself, whether I'm in front of 12 or 200 people.

—Michael Carter, VP and GM of Stryker Medical

If you are interested in taking your leadership to the next level, this is the book to read. Thought-provoking, yet a fun and easy read, it delivers actionable new ideas in every chapter. You'll want everyone you know in a position of influence to read and apply its lessons.

—John Clendening, EVP of Investor Services at Charles Schwab

We spend endless hours growing our skills as leaders but underinvest in communication. This isn't about main stage flash; it's about motivating, inspiring, and influencing others to take action. *Communicate to Influence* isn't about presentation skills; it's about raising the game on how you show up as a leader.

—Katy Keim, Chief Marketing Officer of Lithium

Proven ideas to make you a better speaker in all settings . . . a great book and a fast and fun read! I particularly like the Communicator's Roadmap, which helps you position yourself and your audience so you can ultimately inspire people.

—Paul Hoffman, Retired Software Executive
at Informatica, Oracle, and Documentum

Any leader who wants to create change needs to learn how to Communicate to Influence. Leaders in my organization have benefited from these principles.

—Gunjan Aggarwall, Head of HR and Talent Acquisition at Ericsson

A roadmap for immediate action! *Communicate to Influence* shows us how to step up and inspire. This is a must-read for leaders everywhere.

—John McGee, SVP of Worldwide Sales at FireEye

The lessons in this book can convert an awkward speaker into a compelling communicator. I know because I have seen it happen. Using a handful of key principles, the Decker team transforms stilted, cluttered presentations into dynamic interactive conversations. If you need help with your communications skills, this is the place to start.

—Duncan Simester, NTU Professor of Marketing
at MIT Sloan School of Management

The Deckers nail it. This book gives the latest success principles of the two key elements of speaking: behavior and content. I love the Decker Grid! I use it all the time.

—Lyne Brown, Vice President of eCommerce at The Clorox Company

This book explains the art and science of modern communication . . . how to win people's attention away from time pressures, social media, e-mails, and continuous news feeds. Up-to-date examples and new tools explain ideas that are easy to grasp. It's valuable reading for those of us who need to influence others. I plan to use the Decker Method the next time I deliver a conference keynote.

—Mike Faith, CEO of Headsets.com, Inc.

# COMMUNICATE TO INFLUENCE

## HOW TO INSPIRE YOUR AUDIENCE TO ACTION

BEN DECKER & KELLY DECKER

NEW YORK   CHICAGO   SAN FRANCISCO
ATHENS   LONDON   MADRID
MEXICO CITY   MILAN   NEW DELHI
SINGAPORE   SYDNEY   TORONTO

6  7  8  9  0  QFR   21  20  19  18

ISBN 978-0-07-183983-9
MHID      0-07-183983-6

e-ISBN 978-0-07-183984-6
e-MHID      0-07-183984-4

The Decker Method™, the Communicator's Roadmap™, and the Decker
Grid™ are trademarks of Decker Communications, Inc.

Design by Mauna Eichner and Lee Fukui

McGraw-Hill Education books are available at special quantity discounts
to use as premiums and sales promotions or for use in corporate training
programs. To contact a representative, please visit the Contact Us pages at
www.mhprofessional.com.

*To the founders of Decker Communications, Bert and Deborah Decker. The vision you set forth 36 years ago is forever planted in the Hall of Fame of the Inspire quadrant and continues to transform people's lives. We are humbled and honored to carry it forward today.*

*Deborah (Mom), your spirit lives on in every coaching session. Whether it's a full day or 10 minutes, every client feels—above all—cared for and encouraged.*

*Bert (Dad), thank you for your trust, your challenge, and your endless energy and passion for our work. We are blessed by your faith, wisdom, guidance, and love in all we do.*

# Contents

# Foreword

**was talking to** a group of nonprofit leaders—it was right after lunch, the time slot that every speaker dreads. (You should never try to compete with digestion.) Near the edge of the room, I saw an older gentleman with his arms crossed, eyes closed, and mouth agape—a hair's breadth away from a snore. I couldn't help but smile. (I can appreciate the value of a nap, even at my expense.)

But then I saw a second person whose eyes were drooping. My smile began to fade. Next the phones started surfacing. Popping up like prairie dogs all around the room. Maybe they were eager to tweet my speakerly wisdom? Sadly, no. I'd lost them. Soon I found myself talking to a room full of foreheads, wondering how I could earn back their attention.

The book you're holding is the perfect tool for preventing Forehead Moments. The Deckers have written a guidebook for communicating in a way that inspires an audience.

If you don't know the Deckers' work, you're in for a treat. We have known Ben and Kelly since 2009. (By the way, "we" is Chip and Dan Heath. We started in the first person so Dan could tell his Forehead Moment tale.) We worked with them to create a course—based on our book *Made to Stick*—that has since been delivered in several dozen Fortune 500 companies.

For 36 years, the folks at Decker Communications, founded by Ben's father, Bert, have served as elite coaches for some of the world's top leaders and executives, helping them prepare for critical speeches and presentations. In Silicon Valley, if your tech firm's CEO gets a keynote slot at the Consumer Electronics Show, you know you'd better speed dial the Deckers.

Getting presentation tips from the Deckers is like getting basketball tips from Phil Jackson. They've seen it all and worked with the best. Here are some of the highlights you will encounter in the pages ahead:

- The story of an executive who was so aghast at how he looked on video that he suspected trickery (*Is that really what I sound like??*)

- A discussion of the most common reasons that speakers lose audiences

- Why an executive started a high-stakes speech by admitting she'd lied on her driver's license application

- Why you shouldn't start your talks with an "LBOW" (Lovely Bunch of Words)

- And how the use of a simple grid will forever change the way you prepare for presentations

One of our favorite stories in the book is about a voicemail that was left for Kelly Decker by a clueless sales representative. It's a canned sales pitch, so bad that it's funny. But the Deckers don't share it in order to mock it; they share it in order to transform it. It makes a great "Before" and "After" story, seeing how the sales rep could have reworked that message to *make a connection.* (Here's hoping the salesman gets a copy of this book—he stands to octuple his commissions.)

This book shows that becoming a great communicator takes just two things: a smart game plan and a lot of practice. Turn the page to begin your own transformation.

—Chip Heath and Dan Heath, coauthors of the *New York Times*
bestseller *Made to Stick: Why Some Ideas Survive and Others Die*

# Acknowledgments

To our Decker family: You are the change makers who transform business communication that sucks! You lead with humble confidence. You build relationships. You own it. You are champions of continuous improvement. The fan mail about you that we see from clients will never get old. Thank you for inspiring us every day with your passion and your love of the game.

To our marketing whiz, Dani Janklow (who also moonlights as a marriage counselor): For answering the call with "I want to." We cannot thank you enough for your ideas, energy, snacks, and superhuman ability to translate inspired thoughts into a story on the page.

To our clients: For getting uncomfortable, taking a risk, becoming great, and then coming back for more. You challenge us and stretch us, and we love every minute of it.

To Vivienne Scholl and Jennifer Scrivner: You inspire us with your design! Thanks for making visual sense out of all of our ideas and creating awesome graphics for the book.

To Jim Denney: Thank you for your help throughout this journey. Your words and research helped put the pieces in place.

To our family (all the Deckers, Seefeldts, and Similes) and friends: For your ideas, edits, and advice. For destressing us, encouraging us, and loving us. For saying, "It will be OK"; "The kids will survive"; "We're so proud." Every word, e-mail, thought, and prayer holds us up, and we are grateful.

Above all—and this is more than just an acknowledgment—to our boys, Jackson, Joseph, and Christopher: We love you. Thank you for putting up with the crazy busy times so that we can spend quality time making awesome family memories: fishing, swimming, skiing, and hiking; in the mountains and at the beach; on scooters, bikes, and horseback; and on makeshift baseball diamonds, soccer fields, and basketball courts just about everywhere.

# Introduction:
# Why Influence?

**W**hen you think of powerful business communications, you don't ordinarily think of the military. That's because officers can bark their orders to recruits, and they'll hear a "Yes, sir!"

In working with several branches of the military, it's always interesting when we walk in with our message of moving from information to influence. After all, the military works because of its hierarchical structure and strict obedience to orders. What role does influence play in this kind of environment? We once asked a cadet in the U.S. Coast Guard what it's like—specifically, how he responds to directives. He replied, "This is the military. You do what you're told. But I will tell you this: when I know how my superior officer feels, or why I should follow that order, I know I respond differently, or with a different motivation. It feels like more than just a directive."

The cadet's response shifted from "I have to" to "I want to," all because of a different communication experience that his superior created. Even in the military, there is great power in and opportunity for connection.

Authority is certainly one way to influence. It's tried and true. But it's also tired. It's become synonymous with tyranny and autocracy. Instead, we challenge you to rise above the level of flashing your title to get people to act.

At work, at school, at home, in our communities, and on the sports field, we all have an amazing opportunity to lead by influence, not by authority. In fact, we could even take it one step further and answer a bigger call to Inspire.

Our audience is *begging* to be inspired. And let's face it, when *we're* in the audience, we want to be inspired, too. There's an endless deluge of data, facts, and figures. We're inundated with all of that, and we're seeking more. Trust is down, our attention is spread thin, and we're thirsting for inspiration all around us. Urge us to be part of something. Challenge us to believe in something. Motivate us to act.

In his book *Start with Why*, Simon Sinek writes, "There are leaders and there are those who lead. Leaders hold a position of power or influence. Those who lead inspire us. Whether individuals or organizations, we follow those who lead not because we have to, but because we want to. We follow those who lead not for them, but for ourselves."

For ourselves.

Every person in your audience is thinking, "What can you do for me? How does this relate to me?" And therein lies a great opportunity (one that many of us miss): the opportunity to influence *them*. In this book, we'll introduce the Communicator's Roadmap as your tool to navigate your communication experience intentionally and make it about *them*. You'll learn how to build an emotional connection with those in your audience and create a message that is so relevant to *them* that they can't idly sit by. We'll urge you to move away from the default practice of Informing and instead aspire to Entertain, Direct, and Inspire.

This is a book on speaking. Or, more accurately, it's a book on communicating the spoken word. Lest you think that you are not a public speaker, here's a news flash: *there is no such thing as private speaking!* And while it's true that we may not have formal speaking opportunities going on all the time, each one of us communicates *many* times a day, *every* single day of the week. We are always communicating, and we can practice these principles every day. Even if we are just talking on the phone or in the hallway, we can be aware of *the communication experience* that we are creating for our listeners. But most of the time, we're blissfully *un*aware of it.

Ben remembers one client from when he first started executive coaching—we'll call this client Eric. To be candid, Eric was pretty intimidating on paper. He had an undergraduate degree in computer science from a prestigious Ivy League university, a law degree from Harvard, as well as an MBA. He had been admitted to the bar in three states, and he was a senior executive in a global financial services group. When Ben learned that he would be training Eric, there was definitely a twinge of insecurity: "Who am I to add value to *this* guy?" But after just one meeting, the need for coaching and feedback was clear: Eric was a terrible communicator. Ben's first impression of him was that he was cool and aloof.

But over the next few days, as Ben worked with Eric, he realized that his first impression was a misimpression. Eric wasn't really cool and aloof, just a bit stiff and uncomfortable around people. Ben got to know him fairly well, and he was a really nice guy. The challenge was to help him bring that nice guy to the surface. So Ben worked on his behavior—the way he came across—especially on his smile, eye communication, and gestures. He was eager to learn, and Ben saw a rapid improvement in his ability to deliver a speech. But his transformation didn't stop there.

A few weeks later, one of the other executives in Eric's company asked, "What did you do to Eric?"

A little worried, Ben responded, "Excuse me?"

He said, "Eric's a different person. He's changed."

"You mean as a speaker?"

"I mean as a *person*. He just seems more engaging—more warm and friendly. More likable."

Eric had taken what he had learned and applied it not only to his formal presentations and speeches but also across the board, in his everyday conversations and all his interactions. And people *liked* the new Eric.

Talk about influence! You know it's worth it when you get feedback like that.

Use the Communicator's Roadmap along with the other tools we'll provide in this book, and be intentional about the experiences you create. It can be *transformational* if you let it. You might begin by working to become a better presenter, but you'll soon discover that you're becoming a better leader in your organization, a better partner in your marriage, a better parent to your children, and a better friend to your friends. You will *influence* on a whole new level.

## WHAT ARE YOU WAITING FOR?

Business communication sucks, but there is hope. It doesn't have to be this way. And it can't. Circumstances and our audience demand that it change. The need for great communicators has never been more urgent. There is much to be changed, new ideas to launch, and greater connections to establish. Whether you're a product manager for a tech company, a wholesale broker for an insurance company, or a relationship manager in finance, you have to drive your audience members to action and inspire them to change.

For more than 36 years, Decker Communications has been the leading communications firm helping business leaders communicate in a more influential, connected way. Most of our work is experiential, and it is almost always in person. We use two foundations: video feedback and private coaching. The mission of our company is to transform business communications by identifying the gaps between where communicators are and where they want to be. Then we show them how to get there. In this book, we're putting this experiential approach into writing so that you can get there, too.

The challenge that we won't be able to control is . . . are *you* willing to change? Are you willing to shift your mindset? To alter the way you've always approached communication? To raise your awareness so that you can see what others see? So much of communication is about habits—challenging yourself and taking risks. Some of the ideas in this book will sound risky and may feel crazy to do! But there is much to be gained. Our hope is that this book encourages you to take that leap, so that you, too, will reap the great rewards of influencing your listeners and inspiring them to action. What better time to start than now?

### CHAPTER 1

# Business Communication Sucks

*The two words "information" and "communication"*
*are often used interchangeably, but they signify*
*quite different things. Information is giving out;*
*communication is getting through.*
—Sydney J. Harris

I n 2013, Marissa Mayer was ranked no. 32 on the *Forbes* list of the World's 100 Most Powerful Women. In 2014, she moved up to no. 18 on that list, just below Beyoncé Knowles. Not bad for an engineering nerd.

When Marissa Mayer took the helm as president and CEO of Yahoo! in 2012, the company was seen as a digital media dinosaur whose best days were in the rearview mirror. She quickly changed all that with a website redesign, a host of new products, a series of major acquisitions, including

Tumblr, and a sales force shakeup. Media profiles painted her as "iron-fisted,"[1] "authoritarian," and "a dictator, with a top-down style,"[2] yet she was also glamorized as a tastemaker, even scoring a bold photo spread in *Vogue*. Though she teetered between dorky and chic, nobody could deny that she was getting results. In her first 14 months with the company, Yahoo!'s stock price more than doubled.

Vaulting into the spotlight, she rapidly became a household name and a business icon. If her name was on the marquee, the event would sell out. What would Marissa say? Would we hear her signature snorty laugh? What would she wear? Opportunities were aligning, left and right, for her to share her vision, steer industry conversations, and join influential boards. When she was part of something, people expected great results.

That's why the international community was waiting with bated breath—and active Twitter handles—when she gave a presentation at the 2014 Cannes Lions International Festival of Creativity. Cannes Lions is a conclave of 12,000 advertising and media creators and executives from 94 countries, representing billions of dollars in ad revenue. Presentations at the event highlight the very best work throughout the year, and speakers deliver inspiring, thought-provoking talks about the future of creativity in advertising. It is, after all, *a festival of creativity*. But Mayer didn't get that memo.

Mayer sacrificed connection for content. While other presenters at the event created exciting experiences with unscripted presentations and audience participation, Mayer stayed rooted behind a lectern and read a canned speech from a teleprompter screen. Her performance was described as stiff, forced, and pandering.[3]

Even worse, her scripted content didn't connect. It wasn't inspirational. It wasn't thought-provoking. In fact, her entire message came off as a Yahoo! sales pitch. At Cannes Lions, speakers are expected to be thought leaders, not company or brand leaders. Mayer was skewered by tweets. Business reporter Laura Petrecca of *USA Today* tweeted from the event, "Yahoo CEO @marissamayer puts forth a VERY hard sell of the company during her Tues presentation at the #canneslions ad festival."[4]

Marissa Mayer missed two critical opportunities: (1) she missed the opportunity to be more than a talking head, the opportunity to create a real, emotional connection with her audience that would engender trust and believability, and (2) she missed the opportunity to think beyond a Yahoo! sales pitch and data dump and move toward a bigger message of influence and inspiration. She had a golden moment to spur change and give the audience members goose bumps. Her paramount mistake: she made it all about her, and not at all about them.

Did it end her career? No. Did she earn any new fans or endorsements from the international audience? No. She was OK. But she could have been great. If you were speaking in front of thousands of influential people in the south of France, wouldn't you want to be great?

But the important point here isn't about Marissa Mayer. It's not about a big name, a big event, or a big opportunity. It's about our daily communications—in the morning huddle, the quarterly town hall meeting, the midyear all-hands meeting, the weekly sales call, industry conferences, client pitches, and quarterly business reviews. We approach all of these in the exact same way that Marissa Mayer approached Cannes Lions. We spit out the information we want to share, along with the information we need to share, and we miss the opportunity to influence, inspire, or even mildly entertain because we don't consider the experience that we're creating. We get stuck in an information overload of facts, stats, updates, and action items.

We don't bother to create an emotional connection because it's just too hard, or maybe because we don't dare. We're not intentional about influencing because we don't get close enough to what our audience expects, wants, and needs. We don't show the contagious passion that it takes to ignite action. Instead, we present our agenda and the logical arguments to support it, and then expect our audience to come right along with us. We shortsightedly expect others to take our information the way we present it and then do something with it. In doing so, we perpetuate every single reason that business communication sucks.

So let's do something about it! The first step is to admit that we have a problem. In fact, we consistently tell ourselves five little white lies about our own communications (Figure 1-1) to justify why maybe, just maybe, we don't really suck.

## THE FIVE WHITE LIES ABOUT COMMUNICATION

White Lie #1: If I say the words, people will get it.

White Lie #2: When I'm "on," I'm great.

White Lie #3: I don't need to prep. I can wing it.

White Lie #4: People tell me I'm pretty good at speaking.

White Lie #5: That's not the way we do things here.

Figure 1-1

# WHITE LIE #1: "IF I SAY THE WORDS, PEOPLE WILL GET IT."

Think back to a recent message you delivered—to your executive team, your staff, or a customer or client. What percentage of your time did you spend developing your content versus practicing your delivery? If you're like the people we coach and train every day, you probably spent at least 99.9 percent of your time preparing the content. You scripted or created a very detailed outline (maybe even with bullets!) of an argument, positioned details, layered on data and proof points, carefully crafted transitions, and finally prepared the coup de grâce . . . your PowerPoint deck. All that was left for you to do was to stick to the message.

Let's switch gears for a minute. How many times have you completely tuned out of a meeting because the person who was talking (not you, of course) was boring as hell?

Maybe he spoke in a deathly monotone. Or maybe he showed nervousness in his voice or by wringing his hands. Or maybe he showed a lack of confidence in his, um, I mean, like, the uh . . . story.

What was the difference between your preparation and the horrendous meeting you had to sit through? Nothing. That presenter *was* you. You have—we all have—habits that create an experience. The experience we create either connects with our listeners to draw them in or disconnects and allows them to tune out and start making to-do lists.

Of course, the message is a massive part of that experience, but the most common misconception about communication is the idea that "communication is about words." Communication is not just about words (whether they're on a teleprompter or in a detailed outline); it's about *the experience that you create*. Sticking to the script will not save you, especially when the teleprompter breaks.

Film director Michael Bay is an immensely successful movie director. His credits include *Armageddon* (1998), *Pearl Harbor* (2001), and the *Transformers* series (2007 to the present). As a director, Bay understands that his job is to create an experience for the viewer. Someone should tell him that his job as a public speaker is no different.

On January 6, 2014, Michael Bay took the stage at the five-day Consumer Electronics Show in Las Vegas. Accompanied by Samsung executive Joe Stinziano, Bay's job was to help launch Samsung's new 105-inch ultra-high-definition curved TV. Facing a crowd of hundreds of tech professionals and journalists, he began, "My job as a director is I get to dream for a living—" Then he stopped and nervously rubbed his hands together. An awkward silence ensued.

Stinziano tried to rescue him, asking him a question about moviemaking. Bay said, "I create visual worlds that are so beyond everyone's normal life experiences, and Hollywood is a place that creates a viewer escape. And what I try to do as a director is I try to—"

He trailed off into silence. A pained expression came over his face, and he turned away from the audience with a groan. Then he turned back to the audience and said, "The type is all off, sorry. I'll just wing this."

Stinziano prompted him to continue.

Bay started again. "I try to take people on an emotional ride, and, um—" Again he trailed off into silence.

"The curve?" Stinziano said. "How do you think the curved screen is going to impact how viewers experience your movies?"

"Excuse me," Bay said. "I'm sorry, I'm sorry." And he turned and walked off the stage.

"Okay," Stinziano said, "ladies and gentlemen, let's thank Michael Bay for joining us."

And a smattering of awkward applause echoed in the stunned room.

Michael Bay later blogged, "The teleprompter got lost. . . . I walked off. I guess live shows aren't my thing."[5]

It was a train wreck. It was painful to watch Michael Bay floundering in front of an audience. The event was a costly misstep for Samsung—and it was even costlier for Michael Bay himself. His onstage meltdown was aired repeatedly on network newscasts and went viral. And we're not telling this story to criticize him in any way. Like so many people in the public eye—entertainers, business executives, politicians, and others—he tried to deliver a scripted speech from a teleprompter screen. His hosts at Samsung and the Consumer Electronics Show undoubtedly told him, "You won't have a thing to worry about. Everything you need to say will be right there on the teleprompter. Nothing can go wrong."

You may be thinking, "Phew! Good thing I don't use a teleprompter!" Here's the thing: the teleprompter was not the problem.

The same exact thing happens with scripted outlines in boardrooms and meetings around the world. It happened recently to Charlene, who became a client of ours because of her experience as part of her Fortune 100 company's high-profile executive development program. She was part of a team that was to deliver its project research and recommendations to the CEO and her executive staff. In the final rehearsal, Charlene began reading from her perfectly scripted message, but then she lost her place. Just like Michael Bay, she tried to recover and wing it, but she quickly became scattered and finally threw up her hands and left the room.

When you rely so heavily on a script (or on bullets or on a teleprompter or an outline), you are considering only one side of the experience. You become so focused on specific words and the order in which you say them that you miss the forest for the trees.

You've seen this happen outside of the business world, too. Think about the acceptance speeches at the Academy Awards. There is a huge difference between the Oscar speeches that are read and the ones that are delivered from the heart. When an Oscar winner whips out a list of names, then looks down and races through the thank yous—heaven forbid someone is omitted—it feels as if everyone gets an honorable mention rather than a heartfelt thanks. Contrast that to the emotional impact you felt when the winner shared a story about the sacrifices someone else made to help him be successful (Jared Leto in 2014), about the time someone talked him off the ledge (Hugh Jackman in 2013), that "a beautiful man and a wonderful agent" is not an oxymoron (Gwyneth Paltrow in 1999), about the first person who took a chance on her career (Lupita Nyong'o in 2014), or that the first time she didn't feel it, but this time around it feels *really* good to get validation that the academy likes you (Sally Field in 1985). Those remarks were delivered from the heart, and they just felt different.

*Reality check:* It's time to ditch the script and stop sacrificing connection for content. The experience is more than the message. That message comes through *you*.

## WHITE LIE #2:
## "WHEN I'M 'ON,' I'M GREAT."

Many people make a false distinction between "public speaking" and having a conversation. They think that public speaking is a performance, like playing a role on stage. But why should we put public speaking in a separate category of communication? Is there any such thing as "private speaking"? Of course not—unless you are talking to yourself. If you are having a conversation with even one other person, you are engaging in the public act of speaking.

So don't think of a presentation to an audience as a performance, as a role you are playing. Think of your presentation as a conversation in which you authentically, transparently interact with your audience. Your ability to *simply be yourself* when you speak may make all the difference to you, your audience, and your organization or cause. Great communicators are authentically themselves all the time. This level of authentic communicating has power—even the power to change losers into winners.

Consider this: in the last four presidential elections, the losing candidate was the one who appeared more contrived and unnatural—the one whose formal campaign persona seemed the most *unlike* his informal private demeanor.

The matchups pitted George W. Bush against Al Gore and John Kerry in 2000 and 2004, respectively, and Barack Obama against John McCain and Mitt Romney in 2008 and 2012. Whether you are on the left or the right, try to put partisan politics aside to see the connection between these rivals—and how their carefully controlled, robotic images shaped their campaigns.

More than three months before the 2012 election, *Politico* columnist Maggie Haberman observed, "Voters crave personal connections with candidates—George W. Bush was the person people wanted to drink a beer with, Bill Clinton felt voters' pain."[6]

Spoofed on *SNL* as having less personality and pizzazz than a manila folder, Al Gore bored Americans throughout his campaign. CBS newsman Bob Schieffer said of Gore (who lost in 2000), "I have never known anyone whose off-camera demeanor was so different from what we saw on television. On TV, he seemed stiff and rehearsed, but off it, he was witty and interesting."[7] His behavior was such a contrast with the Gore we've seen since the election—a champion of the environment known for *An Inconvenient Truth*, a nonprofit advocate, and the founder of Current TV.

When John Kerry ran (and lost) in 2004, the PBS documentary series *Frontline* interviewed people who knew Kerry well. The interviewer asked Kerry's older sister Peggy if the real John Kerry was as "aloof" as he so often appeared on television. Peggy Kerry replied, "John, once you get to know him, is really a warm and open and funny human being."[8] The problem is that few people get to know him that way— even those who meet him in person. Pulitzer Prize–winning journalist David S. Rohde once assessed Kerry's persona this way: "When you first meet John Kerry, he can seem as stiff, awkward, and aloof as his television persona—the haughty, flip-flopping Massachusetts aristocrat who lost the 2004 presidential election against an eminently beatable George W. Bush."[9]

Former TV anchor Kathy Kerchner wrote John McCain's political epitaph more than four months before he lost the 2008 election: "In person, and often in interviews and speeches where he's expressing himself extemporaneously, McCain is as charming as Obama. He's funny and self-effacing, authentic, friendly and engaged." But put him in front of an audience with a scripted speech, Kerchner said, "and watch that natural charisma disappear."[10] Many commentators noted that McCain's concession speech was probably the finest speech of his career—a relaxed and humble speech that he delivered when he no longer had anything to lose, and no longer had political handlers telling him what to say and how to say it.

In the 2012 election, Mitt Romney and his handlers deliberately decided to wall off the real Mitt from public view. Romney had an impressive record of good deeds, charitable giving, helping neighbors in need, and saving lives—but his handlers clamped a lid on his personal story out of fear that it would remind voters of his Mormon faith. Many people who knew Romney well described him as warm in person—not at all like the robotic Romney that voters saw on TV.

All of those elections were reasonably close (the 2000 Bush-Gore contest practically came down to a coin flip). If each of the four losing candidates had realized that being "on" turned so many people off, and instead had just been themselves, any one (or maybe even all four) of those elections might have gone the other way.

We see this same political phenomenon when business leaders deliver a formal speech or presentation. They assume an "executive" posture, and they become too polished and overly robotic. As a result, they lose their connection with the audience. And when they lose that, they lose the audience's trust. When you contrast the formal presentation with the off-the-cuff Q&A session, the same person is usually likable, engaging, and connecting. You're great when you're *you*—not when you're "on." In fact, a good red-flag test is to see if there is a difference in the authenticity level of someone onstage and offstage.

*Reality check:* Be authentic—all the time. Audiences want to see and hear the *real* you, so that they can determine whether or not they trust you. The very best communicators don't change from one situation to another. They may dial their voice up or down and use big behaviors onstage, but they are always the same authentic person. And that means it's time to stop "giving speeches," and it's time to become spontaneous, vulnerable, and human.

## WHITE LIE #3: "I DON'T NEED TO PREP. I CAN WING IT."

Many of us have Outlook calendars that are booked back-to-back-to-back. Day after day after day. It makes it pretty tough to prep for our 3 p.m., because we don't have time anywhere else in our day. We've all been there. What happens? We get into the habit of winging it. As leaders, we're lucky in that we can usually get away with it. But the difference between zero preparation and a little bit of focus is much greater than the sum of the two.

In March, Ben got a call from an existing client—we'll call him Steven—who was ready to begin preparing for his company's annual branding conference, an event with millions riding on it. "This year, we're going to outdo everything we've done before. A new venue in New York, more publicity than ever before, performances by Grammy winners, presentations by actors and producers. Now we need to make sure all our execs are just as good!"

Ben and Steven jumped in and began to storyboard the right message for the high-stakes New York event. At the end of their brainstorming, they planned out a series of follow up meetings to further refine the message and to allow for practice, practice, and more practice. As they wrapped up the meeting, Ben asked Steven if there was anything else he had going on.

"Oh," he said, "I've got this little off-site retreat at Auberge in Napa Valley—but it's an internal event, not a big deal. I'm not going to prep much for it. I'll just go in with my agenda, shoot from the hip, make my points, and it'll be fine."

Upon hearing "Auberge," Ben's radar lit up. Auberge du Soleil is one of the top hotels in the world. It's not exactly the place for a no-big-deal kind of meeting. Ben quizzed him further: Who would be there? What was the purpose of the retreat? What were the stakes?

"Well, it's our senior leadership staff," he said. "We're about to take a left turn in our strategy—pretty much 90 degrees from the direction we've been going. We're asking our top people to adjust to some radical new approaches. As for the stakes—well, it's funny you should ask that, because the stakes are pretty high. We need to get buy-in from everybody."

"And what happens if you don't get buy-in from everybody?" Ben asked.

Steven paused. "I hadn't really thought that far ahead. The more questions you ask, the more I realize that this little Napa Valley retreat is just as important—if not more important—for our company's future as the huge branding conference in New York."

"When is this retreat?"

"In three days."

"Well, we'd better get started."

Like so many of us, Steven was focused on communication when the stakes were high. Are only events with bright lights and a big stage prep-worthy? There's nothing like an audience of thousands of people to motivate you to prepare. And yet, we're missing opportunities to influence and inspire everywhere else. Every interaction is an opportunity and worthy of great communicating. When he has an internal meeting coming up, Steven no longer says, "It's not a big deal—I'll just shoot from the hip."

Thomas A. Stewart, the editor of *Harvard Business Review*, put it another way: "Everything a leader does is symbolic. Everything is amplified. 'If the chairman asks for a cup of coffee,' runs an old joke at General Electric, 'someone is liable to go out and buy Brazil.'"[11] Remember that you are always being observed, whether the stakes seem to be high or low. If you're not prepared or you're not paying close enough attention, you might not be communicating what people need to see and hear. And you'll miss opportunities to go from informing to influencing.

*Reality check:* You're always communicating, so it's always worth some preparing. Don't limit great communicating to big events. Good communication habits are for the off-site leadership retreats, the weekly coffee-and-doughnuts staff meetings, the business lunches at the local steakhouse, and even the impromptu conversations in the hallway. (The good news is that this preparation will become easy. We've got a simple, quick tool to help you prepare and frame your message every time. If you want to cut to the chase, go ahead and flip to Chapter 6.)

## WHITE LIE #4: "PEOPLE TELL ME I'M PRETTY GOOD AT SPEAKING."

We have three young boys, and, as you might imagine, story time is a pretty big deal at our house. One of their favorite stories is Hans Christian Andersen's "The Emperor's New Clothes," and it goes something like this:

Once upon a time there was an emperor who cared only about fine clothing. One day, two swindlers came into town and told everyone that they were the most amazing weavers and could create the most magnificent fabrics the land had ever seen, fabric so magnificent that it would become invisible to those who were unfit for their positions. The emperor decided that he must hire these weavers so that he could tell the wise men from the fools. The swindlers agreed to produce their finest suit, in exchange for money, gold thread, and silk. They pocketed the materials and pretended to weave away madly. The fear of being seen as a fool was so strong that even the emperor's most trusted advisor reported that the fabric was the most excellent work he had ever seen. Finally, when the suit was complete, the swindlers pretended to dress the emperor in his new clothes and prepared him for a grand procession. (Enter howling laughter from the boys.) The townspeople smiled, waved, and applauded the emperor until a child pointed and yelled, "But he hasn't got anything on!" When the rest of the town finally began chanting with the child, the emperor's worst suspicions were confirmed, but he completed his prideful procession.

This bedtime story is an analogy for any leader who needs to work on communications. Your team members may be so worried about losing favor that they will offer you a shine job, sugarcoating their feedback rather than actually sharing what you need to hear. Fortunately, there is one great instrument for eliciting honest feedback: a video recording.

The CEO of a $30 million software start-up came to Ben for some coaching in preparation for another round of venture funding. He had founded the company with his brother just three years earlier. He was the older of the two, in his early thirties, and he was definitely the intense one—logical with a healthy dose of skepticism. Ben asked him, "Have you ever seen yourself on video before?" The CEO said no, he hadn't. So we had him give a five-minute presentation in front of a video camera. His voice had almost no inflection, and his expression was flat. He projected overconfidence to the point that he came across as cool and aloof.

We sat down with him and played back his performance in high definition. About 30 seconds into the playback, he said, "Whoa! Hold it! Pause it, please!"

Ben paused the playback.

"Let me understand something," the CEO said. "As I'm watching myself on video, is that the same as you seeing me give the presentation live?"

"I'm not sure I follow your question," Ben said. "But if you're asking me whether what I'm seeing on the TV screen is exactly what I saw and heard when I recorded you live, then yes, I'd say it's the same thing."

His eyes widened and his jaw dropped. "So, what I'm hearing now is how people always hear my voice?"

"Yup."

"That's how I sound?"

"Yup."

He was silent for a few seconds—then said, "That's fucked!"

"Yup."

He was experiencing the disorientation of seeing himself on video for the first time. This experience is called *disparity*. It's the discovery that the way we *think* we come across to others is completely different from the way we *actually* come across to others. One of the most common problems top executives have is that no one dares give them honest feedback. No one dares to say, "Boss, you really stink at this!" Instead, people sugarcoat it: "Great job—that was awesome!" Or, in many cases, they say nothing at all.

That's why video feedback can come as a huge shock to leaders—video sometimes reveals that the emperor has no clothes. Many businesspeople go through their careers thinking, "I'm a good enough communicator to get by." They have no idea what their communication habits and idiosyncrasies are. They've never seen themselves in action. They think they're doing fine, when they are actually hurting themselves and their organizations. The good news is that this initial realization, as painful as it may be, leads to major improvements in their communication skills. Let the video be a mirror for your communications.

*Reality check:* You can't create a communication experience for your audience until you become self-aware. This means getting communication coaching and feedback—especially video feedback. It also means seeking feedback from your peers regularly and creating a culture of sharing feedback across your team.

## WHITE LIE #5: "THAT'S NOT THE WAY WE DO THINGS HERE."

Many leaders within organizations and corporate businesses aren't excellent communicators, and we see a trickle-down effect. After years of watching her boss read from behind the lectern, or editing PowerPoint decks filled with bullet points, jargon, and footnotes for her senior executives to share, a midlevel manager says, "I am going to be that way, present that way, because that's obviously what it takes to get to that level." The result is often an organization or a business with average or below average communicators. And thus . . . the title of this chapter.

Think about mirroring, the classic act of doing what the person you are talking to does. If he changes his body language, you change your body language. While this technique is often used in sales situations, consider this: If the other person is boring, serious, and showing a lack of interest with a slouch, should you be boring, serious, and also show a lack of interest with a slouch? No way! That's a sad, vicious cycle.

Change is never easy, and it's even harder when you're the one who's leading the charge. You stand out, and you are different from the rest of the team. It feels so much riskier, and it almost doesn't make sense—it goes against logic and reason—to do something differently.

Recently we conducted a series of training programs with a group of business unit vice presidents from a large insurance company based in Illinois. Each VP had been with the company for more than 15 years, knew its ins and outs, had received mentoring by other leaders in the company, and had relocated several times for various leadership positions. These people were viewed as the company's future top leaders. The executive sponsor of the training program had an interesting request of us: "We're leaning on you to help change our culture. It's too stiff, meetings are too long and ineffective, and things just aren't getting done the way they could be. We're facing big changes and challenges in the next year, and we need to do things differently. These leaders need to be excellent, energizing communicators. We need your help to give them a green light to take more risks—and they're likely to resist because of the culture."

Sure enough, we had our work cut out for us. We urged the VPs to get out of their shells to show passion, to connect with and energize their teams. They resisted because the new practices felt awkward and uncomfortable. That didn't surprise us—it's hard to get out of your comfort zone! What surprised us was that they actually said: "This is not the way we do things here."

The breakthrough happened when we told them about the permission and approval from the executive team. They needed to hear that it was OK to take a risk, to change their style and approach to communicating. Suddenly, something shifted, almost as if a light went on above their heads. They responded with, "If you look around the organization, the people who are moving up and being promoted are the ones doing some of these things: showing more emotion, more passion, mixing things up. I'll try it." Needless to say, the rest of the training went well. And as they shifted their communication styles, it made a dent in the shift of culture inside this rather large company. Their new behaviors, stories, and real-life examples resuscitated those meetings. And it all stemmed from the moment they gave themselves permission to change.

*Reality check:* It doesn't have to be the way it has always been. In fact, it can't be! Don't let yourself fall prey to Einstein's definition of insanity: doing the same thing but expecting different results. Instead, use storyteller Doug Stevenson's mantra, "Safe is a dangerous place to be." Be bold and get out of your comfort zone to inspire others to more: more ownership, more buy-in, more empowerment.

## YOUR CHARGE: CHANGE THE STATUS QUO

Business communication sucks. Stop being part of the problem by lying to yourself. A quick reality check will show you that everything that's wrong with business communication today can be made right—with a few simple yet powerful tools. You are called to communicate well. This call has never been more urgent. Read on.

---

# EXERCISES

---

**WATCH**

- Watch the next award show (or at least the best and worst speech highlights). Check out the huge differences in the acceptance speeches.

- Look for the differences in executive presentations during your next town hall meeting, sales kickoff, or industry conference. Who's scripted?

---

**THINK**

- Which white lies are you most guilty of?

- When do you turn "on" and "off"? How would your family or friends describe you? How would your colleagues describe you?

- How much time do you spend preparing your message versus practicing your delivery?

- For what situations do you prepare the most?

- What feedback have you received about your communications?

---

**DO**

- Get a video recording of yourself. Stat. You'll need it soon.

---

### CHAPTER 2

# On Deaf Ears

*Every improvement in communication*
*makes the bore more terrible.*
—FRANK MOORE COLBY

**W**hat if almost half of *everything* you say isn't getting through? Actually, if you have young kids, as we do, you're probably thinking that about half of it getting through is pretty darn good. Well, maybe it's debatable that it's okay when you're dealing with kids (although we actually don't think so), but it definitely is not debatable when you're dealing with adults in today's cacophonous, crowded, cluttered communications world. Not if you want to accomplish something.

Think about this: You're desperately trying to sell an idea, pitch a product, change a process, or gain some attention in a crowded market. You're speaking. They're not listening. We now have extreme expectations for communications. How did we get here? Where did these expectations come from? We can pinpoint three societal trends that are giving communicators a swift kick in the rear to change:

1. The entire landscape of trust has shifted. There's an ever-increasing trust gap between us and our leaders. When we don't trust people, their communications fall on deaf ears.

2. We live in an attention economy, but we're communicating with foreign currency. If we can't get their attention, there aren't even any ears to land on.

3. A backlash against information overload has left us thirsting for inspiration. We don't want a checklist; we want to be called to something greater. When we're not, we can't separate the signal from the noise.

It's absolutely critical for you to understand these trends to help you navigate your journey. We must *earn the right to be heard*. Let's start with trust.

On April 30, 2014, CNN broke the story that at least 40 U.S. veterans had died while waiting for appointments at the Veterans Health Administration facility in Phoenix. Within days, reports of similar neglect at other VHA facilities around the country surfaced. Whistle-blowers came forth, saying that VHA administrators and staffers were "cooking the books," falsifying records to hide treatment delays.

On May 15, Veterans Affairs Secretary Eric Shinseki went before the Senate Veterans' Affairs Committee to testify about the mushrooming scandal. General Shinseki read a prepared statement, saying that the news of neglect of U.S. veterans by his agency "makes me mad as hell." However, though General Shinseki's words were tough, his voice was flat, his face expressionless.

Days after General Shinseki's testimony, Jon Stewart of *The Daily Show* mocked the general's testimony, saying to General Shinseki, "Your 'mad-as-hell' face looks a lot like your 'oh-we're-out-of-orange-juice?' face."[1] Stewart was expressing what many Americans felt: a sense of distrust of the general's lukewarm performance. One congressman echoed that sentiment, saying, "It has become clear that [General Shinseki] has lost the trust of the public."[2]

General Shinseki didn't lose the people's trust just because veterans were being neglected on his watch. He lost the people's trust because his "mad as hell" performance was unconvincing. To be fair, the general was probably every bit as sincere and upset as he claimed to be. After all, he is a veteran of two combat tours in Vietnam and was awarded three Bronze Stars for valor and a Purple Heart after losing part of his foot to a land mine. The idea that he was indifferent to the needs of our veterans is inconceivable.

But General Shinseki didn't understand that he was unconvincing. In Chapter 1, we said that *every* communication counts. We must earn trust every time we speak. Though Shinseki desperately wanted to keep his job and fix the problems at the VHA, he had squandered that precious commodity called *trust*. On May 30, under enormous public and political pressure, he resigned. In the end, his lackluster performance at the hearing was nearly as damning as the scandal itself and directly contributed to his departure. Trust must be earned, and there was a widening trust gap between General Shinseki and the American people.

You're probably thinking, "There's certainly no shortage of examples of lack of trust in government—or its leaders." Indeed, it would be easy to put the government trust issue on the shelf and move on, but the trust gap extends far beyond the government and the military. This trust gap plagues leaders at every level, whether in sports, entertainment, or business at large. Scandals surround our everyday lives, from fraudulent accounting, to steroid abuse, to privacy infringements. Trust in traditional leadership sources has evaporated. This trust gap is one of the new and unyielding realities of communicating in the twenty-first century, and it's dramatically shifting the way we think about and respond to traditional sources of power.

## THE TRUST GAP HAS FLIPPED POWER AND AUTHORITY

The global market research firm Edelman Berland publishes an annual report, the *Edelman Trust Barometer*, that measures public confidence in the leaders of both business and government. Every year since 2009, the *Trust Barometer* has found that public confidence has been critically low. What happened to cause this crisis of confidence? The global financial crisis of 2008, triggered by the subprime mortgage crisis. We're not going to drag you back into those weeds of fraudulent underwriting, predatory lending, regulatory malpractice, and federal agency woes, but here's the gist: the public lost trust in the business sector. It was the worst financial meltdown since the Great Depression, and the public concluded that a combination of private-sector greed and government inattention nearly collapsed the world economy. Bye-bye, trust in business; bye-bye, trust in government.

The result of this crisis of confidence, says CEO Richard Edelman, is a widening "trust gap" between the American people and their leaders. "Less than one-fifth of the general public believes business leaders and government officials will tell the truth when confronted with a difficult issue," he writes. Edelman goes on to say, "There also is a growing trust gap between institutions and their leaders—globally, trust in business is 32 points higher than trust in business leaders to tell the truth; trust in government is 28 points higher than it is for government officials." (See Figure 2-1.)

In other words, people have far more trust in businesses and government institutions than they have in the *leaders* of those institutions.

If the people you lead don't trust you, then they won't listen to you, they won't be influenced by you, they won't support your agenda, and they won't follow you. In order to lead, you must earn the confidence, trust, and support of the people you lead. If you want to sell people a product, earn their vote, or persuade them of the importance of your cause—and if you're reading this, you do—it's going to be a tough sell. It's much tougher than it was 5 or 10 years ago. And it's only getting more difficult. People no longer trust you simply on the basis of your leadership position. In fact, they may view you and your message with *heightened* skepticism *because* you are in a leadership role. This means that, as leaders, we must also change our approach.

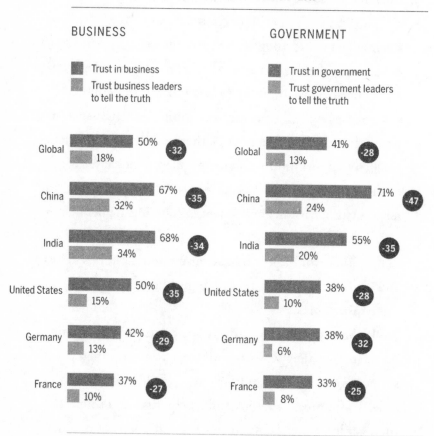

**LEADERSHIP TRUST GAP**

Figure 2-1

Richard Edelman suggests that the solution is for leaders and institutions to adopt a new standard. He calls the old standard of leadership "the License to Operate," and he defines this standard as the freedom to sell products, to raise funds, and to make a profit. The business sector squandered this freedom by driving the global economy to the brink of collapse. Government, with its polarization between the ideologues of the left and those of the right, is incapable of responding to these problems. Since the leaders of government and business have failed to fix these problems, people have revoked the License to Operate of both government and business leaders.[3]

Having lost confidence in government and business leaders, we turn to friends, family, employees, and others like us for information and opinions that we can trust. No longer trusting leaders, or even the brands they represent,[4] we have become our own agents of change, taking to social media for everything from massive social and political movements like Occupy Wall Street and the Arab Spring to everyday travel experiences (enter TripAdvisor, Yelp, and Airbnb).

What does this mean? It means that influence—which used to flow in one direction, from government leaders and business leaders down to the general population—is now dispersed and diffused. Trust and credibility are no longer automatically attached to a leadership position. Jeffrey Sonnenfeld, professor and dean at Yale University, writes, "Reliant, but sidetracked leaders have learned, they cannot rely on their prominent roles or ideas alone to win over key constituents.

Grounded Leadership builds legitimacy in key constituent groups and is based in personal dynamism, empathy, authenticity, inspirational goals and courage."[5] We want to hear directly from employees as ambassadors for the company—to attest to its integrity, its quality and relevance, and its operational strength and leadership.[6]

It's time to rip up that License to Operate. Julie Moreland, president of PeopleClues, contrasts the old-style authoritarian chief executive with today's CEOs, who lead by inspiring, influencing, and motivating, "There is finally room at the top for a new word: 'Influencer.'" Nearly extinct, she says, is the stereotypical top-down boss—the "cigar-chomping, hard-charging guy in suspenders barking out orders," the leader whose authority was based on this template: "A title, strategic directives, meetings, and a 'management' mindset of supervising people and projects."[7]

This is important for all of us to realize: that, regardless of whether or not we hold an "official" title of authority, we must engender trust not only to accomplish our tasks but to lead in our roles. So if you are working in a highly matrixed organization or in a shared services role, you are called upon to lead by influence, not by authority, every day. Many of our clients come to us to help their team members who must influence strategy, key decisions, products, and solutions without having the official authority to do so. We must all *earn* what Edelman calls "the License to Lead," and the key to earning that license is *communication*.

Upon examining specific actions that CEOs can take to build trust, the 2014 study found that communicating clearly and transparently, telling the truth regardless of how complex or unpopular it is, engaging with employees regularly, and being visible during challenging times were critically important to respondents.[8]

Now there's just one little problem: we need to get their attention.

## WE LIVE IN AN ATTENTION ECONOMY, BUT WE'RE COMMUNICATING WITH FOREIGN CURRENCY

In a 2013 business feature, the *Washington Post* described Amazon.com founder Jeff Bezos as a genial yet demanding CEO—and a man with no patience for time wasters: "Amazon employees quickly learn when they have overtaxed the attention of their chief executive. He quietly pulls out his smartphone and starts replying to e-mails. In extreme cases, Bezos will walk out."[9]

Whenever you speak to an audience, imagine a roomful of Jeff Bezoses. Heck, imagine a roomful of other people exactly like you! We are all busy, with deadlines, long to-do lists, and a gazillion digital options competing for our attention. Our smartphones and social media usage have changed the way we listen. In just a few short years, we have become far less willing to simply sit in a chair listening to someone give a speech.

If you've done a lot of public speaking over the past 5 to 10 years, you've probably noticed the change: instead of seeing faces looking up at you, you're seeing a lot of people staring down at their gadgets. Attention spans are shorter, and people are addicted to that little endorphin rush they get when someone likes, shares, or retweets their comment or status.

We're in a new and different communication era, and there's no point in grumbling that our listeners ought to put down their phones and pay attention. They won't—unless we give them good reason to do so. We've got to be more fascinating than the content on their handheld devices—and more fascinating than *any* of the information they could be seeking there. From fact checking to status updating to schedule squeezing, photo editing, bill paying, house hunting, and stock trading, those in your audience can now be doing just about anything other than listening to you.

Of course, if you ask them, "Are you listening?" they'll say, "Sure, I was listening—I can multitask." Yeah, right. Multitasking is a myth. The human mind can focus its attention on only one thing at a time. According to John Medina, a developmental molecular biologist and the author of *Brain Rules*, people who appear to be good at multitasking actually have good working memories that are capable of paying attention to several inputs at one time. Here's the bad news: studies show that a person who is interrupted takes up to 50 percent longer to accomplish a task and makes up to 50 percent more errors.[10] So, if people in your meeting are checking e-mail or tweeting, they are missing something, period.

Business and management researchers Thomas H. Davenport and J. C. Beck define *attention* as "focused mental engagement on a particular item of information. Items come into our awareness, we attend to a particular item, and then we decide whether to act."[11] Your listeners' limited attention span is the gateway—or the bottleneck—for your message. If your listener shuts off her attention, you might as well be talking to a brick wall. Your message cannot reach your listener's awareness—and if you can't get through, forget about motivating your listener to action.

In *The Economics of Attention*, Richard A. Lanham explains, "We live in an 'information economy.' But information is not in short supply in the new information economy. We're drowning in [information]. What we lack is the human attention to make sense of it all."[12] Human attention is a scarce resource—and as more and more information floods our society, the commodity of human attention grows scarcer day by day.

Not to mention that we are battling a serious *device dependency*, from the boardroom to the bedroom to the bathroom. A *Time* poll from 2012 revealed that 84 percent of us could not go a single day without our phones, and 20 percent check a mobile device every 10 minutes.[13] To round out the picture, a 2012 Mobile Mindset Study showed that 54 percent of respondents said that they check their phones while lying in bed: before they go to sleep, after they wake up, or even in the middle of the night. And nearly 40 percent check their devices while on the toilet.[14]

There is so much information at our fingertips. The real question is, where aren't we getting distracted?

Your mission is to cut through the electronic clutter. You have to make yourself more fascinating and compelling than the words and images that flit across the glowing screen of the tablets and smartphones. Don't give your listeners a chance to turn away from your message. Rivet their attention from the word "go." Hold their attention right through to the end of the meeting or until the standing ovation. Here's how one of our clients tests her success: "I know I've done a great job as a communicator when I see eyeballs during my presentation and not the tops of heads."

*Earn the right to be heard.*

## AS A BACKLASH TO INFORMATION, WE WANT INSPIRATION

How can we become more fascinating, more compelling than any of the other distractions echoing around us? At a time when we don't really trust the voices from the megaphones or microphones, and we're inundated with more information than we have time to pay for, what is it that will really catch our attention? What do we crave more than anything else? We want inspiration. We are thirsting for inspiration.

Millennials have made it clear that they thirst for inspiration. According to 2013 reports, 85 percent of millennials want work that makes a difference and is not only enriching to themselves, but also enriching to the world; 71 percent of them want to work for a company or entity that encourages some form of global or community social responsibility. While millennials are low on the totem pole now, they are climbing the ranks, and by 2025 they will make up 75 percent of the global workforce.[15]

And though the "inspire me" banner might be held by millennials, they're not the only ones who are looking to feel something and be part of something bigger. On the other end of the spectrum are baby boomers who are nearing retirement and reflecting on their lives, careers, and purpose. They want to be sure that they've left the world a better place. This collective craving for inspiration is all around. It's contagious. And it results in action.

In his brilliant book *Drive*, Daniel Pink shatters traditional sources of motivation. Instead of the old carrot-and-stick approach to motivation, he asserts that the corporate world would do well to focus on a tripod of three elements that drive us today: autonomy, mastery, and purpose. It is the purpose motive that balances the other two. "Autonomous people working toward mastery perform at very high levels. But those who do so in the service of some greater objective can achieve even more."[16] Purpose doesn't toss profit to one side, but it makes darn sure it has equal footing in the motivation equation.

Where can we see this immediately? In products with purpose and social entrepreneurship. It's the reason that

TOMS Shoes became so popular—not because they were a fashion statement, but because they were a social statement. Founder Blake Mycoskie (who is, not so surprisingly, a fabulous communicator and the author of *Something That Matters*) created a philanthropic for-profit business that started by selling shoes made of recycled, vegan, sustainable materials. Sounds good for the environmentally conscious, but that's not what propelled TOMS. It was the company's purpose: One for One. For every pair of shoes TOMS sold, it would give away another pair of shoes to a child in need. It gives shoes to people who need them! When you buy new ones! This is an idea that resonated and gave people a sense of meaning. It's an idea with which we can connect; it's one that we want to share, whether in person or across any gazillion of our social platforms; and it satisfies a human need: to be part of something bigger. TOMS has since expanded its One for One mantra to eyewear, and TOMS Roasting Co. provides a week of clean water for every purchase of a bag of coffee.

We are desperately seeking inspiration. Fortunately for us, there's a repository of it available for free online. If there is one cultural phenomenon in the past few decades that has answered the bold call for inspiration and transformed the way people communicate, it is TED.

TED (Technology, Entertainment, and Design) is a nonprofit organization that brings together thought leaders from around the world, inviting them to share bold new ideas on everything from science and technology to philosophy and the environment, delivered in a mind-blowing, gut-busting, tear-jerking, thought-provoking 18-minute (or less) talk. Using the slogan "Ideas Worth Spreading," TED has skyrocketed in influence since the first TED event in 1984 and is now a permanent fixture in our culture. Six talks were posted online in June 2006, and they had gained 1 million views by September of that same year. Just six years later, they had gained a billion views. There are now more than 1,700 talks on ted.com, and TED curator Chris Anderson says that TED Talks are viewed more than 2 million times daily.[17]

So what's all the fuss? Why the popularity? Here's what works about TED: it's a format that inspires people. And it landed right smack dab in a desert where we're thirsting for it. Every day we muddle through back-to-back meetings filled with data dump after data dump, resulting in a hopeless list of action items. Enter the TED Commandments, the set of speaker rules that were handed to the very first TED speakers. These rules fly in the face of every conference or corporate presentation ever delivered in the history of meetings, rules that include: "Thou Shalt Reveal Thy Curiosity and Thy Passion," "Thou Shalt Not Flaunt Thine Ego," "Be Thou Vulnerable," "Speak of Thy Failure as Well as Thy Success," and "Thou Shalt Not Read Thy Speech."

During novelist Amy Tan's 2008 TED Talk, "Where Does Creativity Hide?" she shared her reaction to the commandments, joking that the list was "actually something that creates a near-death experience. But near-death is good for creativity." It is a set of rules that would surely send most of us into a tailspin way outside of our comfort zone.

And yet, even the most "corporate" corporations have embraced that discomfort. We see the proliferation of the "TED effect" every day. Our clients come to us more now than they did just two or three years ago, specifically looking for ways to inspire. They need a map that will move them from information to inspiration at their next town hall meetings, sales kickoffs, company retreats, and industry conferences.

The Hertz Corporation, a 96-year-old car rental company with international locations in 145 countries, now holds "TOM Talks." According to CEO Mark Frissora, TOM, which stands for Total Open Mind, is Hertz's shorthand for "an entrepreneurial, innovation orientation," and he and his management team are responsible for driving it through the organization. One way they do it? Through TOM Talks. The executive team selects four people worldwide to deliver an inspiring message in 12 minutes or less at their annual leadership conference. It's now one of the most popular parts of their program.

Take Robert Half International, a 66-year-old human resources consulting company that slashed the duration of the talks its corporate executives gave, leaving them no time for a data dump! The new extreme expectations for presentations are transforming the very experience of meetings.

It's time to move beyond information. Inspiration actually produces a completely different response from the audience.

When you inspire people, it is much easier to persuade them to buy into your vision and goals. In fact, they will move from a position of "have to" to "want to." They will become evangelists for your ideas and help you spread the news far beyond your own reach. If you want to engineer change, if you want your thoughts and views to be adopted by masses of people, then you've got to become a communicator of ideas. The TED slogan, "Ideas Worth Spreading," should become your personal mantra.

## WHAT GOT YOU HERE
## WON'T GET YOU THERE

These societal trends result in extreme expectations for our communications. This is the new landscape that we, as communicators, face. Plain and simple. Your old communication skill set may have gotten you where you are, but those skills will not take you where you want to go. Your words will fall on deaf ears.

We have entered a new era of communication and attention. You now have to earn the right to be heard, and your charge is to take those in your audience from feeling that they "have to" do what you ask to feeling that they "want to" do what you propose. It's time for transformation, and that means it's time for you to go beyond merely informing your listeners. Get ready to influence and inspire them.

# EXERCISES

**WATCH**

- Watch a TED Talk once a week (visit www.ted.com/). You'll find playlists by specific topics, interests, and speakers. Pick your inspiration for the day. The site even includes "Five Talks to Cheer You Up on a Bad Day."

- Look for eyeballs during your next presentation. Or are you only seeing the tops of their heads?

**THINK**

- Whom do you trust? Media? One news network over another? Peer reviews? Friends? Experts? Salespeople?

- What makes you skeptical of those sources?

- Think about your own attention span. How long does it take you to tune out of a meeting? Observe how long it takes before you pull out your mobile device and start multitasking.

**DO**

- Begin your next meeting by asking everyone to put his smartphone out of reach.

- Shorten the time of your next presentation by five minutes to cater to the attention economy.

- Present a bigger vision in your next meeting, rather than defaulting to a tactical explanation.

# Creating a Communication Experience

*They may forget what you said, but they will never
forget how you made them feel.*

—CARL W. BUECHNER

**R**estaurateur Danny Meyer is founder and CEO of the
Union Square Hospitality Group, which includes Union
Square Cafe, Gramercy Tavern, Blue Smoke, Shake Shack, and
many other famous New York City eateries. He's also the author of *The Union Square Cafe Cookbook, Second Helpings from
Union Square Cafe,* and *Setting the Table.* Meyer is in great demand as a public speaker, but it's not his speaking ability that's
important here. It's his approach to designing a restaurant.

In an interview with John Vanderslice of Hilton Worldwide, Meyer explained his philosophy of hospitality. A
restaurant, Meyer said, is not primarily about the food—it's

about the *experience*. The restaurateur's job is not just to serve a great meal. Rather, his job is "creating an experience where each guest really believes you're on their side, that you're doing things for them . . . [so that] when the guests leave, no matter how much money they've spent, they say, 'That was a good use of my time.'"[1]

Creating an experience means *touching the emotions* of the customer. Meyer says that he recruits employees who will make an emotional connection with the customer. He explained, "We're constantly looking for better servers so people will say 'My server made me feel better.' . . . The people we hire . . . are people who are at their happiest when they're making other people feel good."[2] He elaborated, "What do I look for in the people we hire? It's 49 parts how good they are at what they do; 51 parts how important it is to them to make other people feel good. It's a simple recipe, but simple is hard."[3]

Danny Meyer's success in the restaurant business has prompted him to start a new company called Hospitality Quotient. There he teaches his philosophy of creating an experience for the customer. His clients at Hospitality Quotient are companies that are "the best in the world at what they do," and he teaches them to become "the best in the world at how they make people feel."[4] In other words, he teaches companies how to create an experience and make an emotional connection through hospitality.

Meyer sees his mission as a restaurateur as one of meeting basic, primal needs. He explains, "Within five minutes of being born, each of us gets our first four hospitality gifts—eye contact, a smile, a hug, and some pretty good food. Don't think for a moment we don't go searching for those same gifts in every subsequent transaction of our lives."[5]

What does the restaurant business have to do with communicating? If food is only part of the equation for a restaurant, then communication is a whole lot more than just the words you say. It's up to you to create a *communication experience*. And, whether you like it or not, you are *always* creating an experience. You control both what your audience feels and what it remembers. Are people bored or energized? Checked out or interested? Concerned or confident? You also have the opportunity to rally your listeners to gain their trust and leave them saying, "That was a good use of my time." Or, maybe not. Their experience is *in your hands*.

## THE COMMUNICATOR'S ROADMAP

How do we create an ideal communication experience for our audience? We begin by understanding what experience we are creating as communicators and by becoming focused and intentional about that experience. We need a navigational tool to help us get where we want to be. Now, a GPS or your smartphone is only as good as its inputs: your starting point and your destination. Seems basic, right? You just pull up Google Maps so that it can figure out where you are, and then you let it know where you're going . . . voilà!

Unfortunately, it's not so easy for communicators. First, because of all the little lies we covered in Chapter 1, we often don't even know where our starting point is. And second, we're not intentional about our destination. If you're navigating to a new location, you wouldn't dare leave the house without a specific address or the name of your destination. You can't pull a Liz Lemon (Tina Fey's character from *30 Rock*) and just tell Google, "I want to go to there." And yet, we'll walk into a meeting with our prepared agenda but not consider for one second how the team members will react to what we say or how we'll motivate them to action. We just wander in and expect results.

We must treat every communication situation like a new location, and input the destination of where we want to go. Let's break down the Communicator's Roadmap (Figure 3-1).

## The Vertical Axis:
## Creating an Emotional Connection

The vertical axis graphs our emotional connection with our audience. We're not talking tears and heartache here. Emotional connection does not mean being emotional. This emotional connection is what determines whether or not people like us, trust us, and want to follow us. If there is emotional distance, which occurs when we fail to create this connection, our audience will be disinterested or disengaged. This is the result of *low emotional connection*. The higher we are on this axis, the more likable, engaging, warm, and trusted we are.

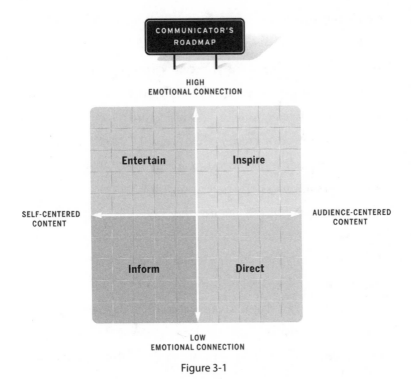

Figure 3-1

Consider some of the speakers you have recently heard. Did they make you laugh, wince, or feel *anything*? Or nothing? If the answer is nothing, you probably didn't really like them, even if you had to listen to them. You were probably bored. At the opposite end of the spectrum, if you were emotionally connected to the speakers, you liked them, trusted them, related to them, wanted to be around them, laughed with them, or at least wanted to keep listening to them.

Who is the boss, leader, or mentor that you admire? For Kelly, "It's Robin MacGillivray, now a retired AT&T executive who ran just about every organization within the business over the course of her 35 years with the company. My

first job out of college was with AT&T (then SBC) as part
of its Leadership Development Program, a rotation-based
program for high-potential recent college grads. I hit the
jackpot with my first rotation. While others in my program
were climbing telephone poles with technicians in the broil-
ing summer heat of Fresno, California, I landed in sales operations, providing communications support to Robin's
2,500-person small business organization (at the cushy headquarters in San Ramon, California). Nice digs, but I was still
the lowest woman on the totem pole. Robin was the highest.

"I'll never forget the first kickoff event I helped coordinate for her and her leadership team at the Westin Bonaven-
ture Hotel in Los Angeles. After a full day of rehearsals and
finalizing details prior to Day 1 of the event, I headed back
through the lobby to my room and ran into Robin. I planned
on just smiling, waving, and moving on. Instead, she stopped
me in my tracks and asked, 'Do you want to grab a cheese-
burger? I'm starving.'

"*With me?* I thought. *I suppose she wants to ask me about
the details of the event.* We sat in the lobby restaurant and or-
dered, and she started asking questions. Except not one of
the questions was about the event. She asked about me. Not
my job, me. And then she shared stories about her own tri-
umphs and tumbles when she started with the company right
out of college. We met a couple of times a year from then on,
and she always made the emotional connection: she showed
that she cared and was interested, and she made it about me."

So how can we make the emotional connection using communication? Two ways:

1. By connecting through behavior: showing that we engage with others to deliver a message; the way that we show warmth, care, and interest, as well as competence.

2. By adding emotion to our content. Our messages must have a logical flow; they must be well structured and well organized. But to create an emotional connection, we need stories, analogies, and even humor in our messages. Stories, especially those that reveal personal vulnerability, help us get to know that person and further increase that connection, just as Robin did.

## The Horizontal Axis: What's the Focus of Our Content?

The horizontal axis represents our content, the actual message that we deliver. This is the part of the Communicator's Roadmap that considers the words you say. Are you distributing information, or are you driving action?

The left side of the axis is reserved for information sharing. If the content is totally focused on *your* agenda, *your* ideas, and *your* goals, if you are constantly saying, "I, I, I," then you'll find yourself at the left end of the horizontal axis. This is self-centered content (you aren't, necessarily, but your content is). The more you are able to focus your content and make it audience-centered—serving the wants, needs, desires, goals, and priorities of the *audience* (however many people that might be, whether it's one or one hundred)—the more you shift the experience to the right side of the horizontal axis. The right side of this axis is action-oriented, and it is the part of the Communicator's Roadmap from which influence flows.

Here's how this plays out in real life: a *typical* product manager talks about a new product by focusing on the facts, features, big wins, and data points; he's always selling it, both internally and externally. That's common, accepted, and expected. He is representing his product. A *great* project manager talks about what her new product means for users and how it will benefit them in their daily lives, for sales teams as they strive to meet their quarterly sales goals, and for fellow product teammates as they develop new elements for the product. Can you see the difference? By shifting the focus to the needs and wants of your audience, you can create a communication experience where those in your audience are motivated to *do* something.

Audience-centered content transforms the whole experience. You'll influence the people in your audience and motivate them to action—and *action* is what communication is all about.

## The Quadrants

With the axes in place, let's look at the resulting communication experiences in each quadrant. As we go through each, think about where you would map your own experiences, either those that you've personally created or those that you've enjoyed (or endured) from others. What quadrant would characterize the last time one of your colleagues led a team meeting, shared an analysis, pitched a product, or made a recommendation? And what quadrant were you in when you did the same?

### Lower Left: Inform

Let's start with the most common quadrant, pretty much the de facto standard for corporate meetings. If you have a *low emotional connection* with your audience and your content is *self-centered*, then you are in the lower left-hand quadrant, along with many others who are simply *informing* the audience. We report, we share a status, we give an update, we provide the details of our research, but we don't connect.

The most iconic example of a speaker with low emotional connection and self-centered content is actor Ben Stein as the droning economics teacher in *Ferris Bueller's Day Off*. If you've seen the film, you'll never forget the bored faces of the students and the teacher's mind-numbing line, "Bueller? . . . Bueller?" Did you know that researchers in Ireland have linked boredom to a monotone voice?[6] This is the epitome of *low emotional connection.* Also consider American journalist and legendary news anchor Dan Rather; congressional leaders Harry Reid, Mitch McConnell, and John Boehner; Major League Baseball commissioner Bud Selig; and former chairman of the Federal Reserve Alan Greenspan (see Figure 3-2). In your everyday life, this is your boring teacher, preacher, or business leader who reads speeches or lectures, and before you know it, you've checked out.

Figure 3-2

### Upper Left: Entertain

This is the quadrant for a person that everyone loves. If you have a *high emotional connection* with your audience but your content is *self-centered*, then you are in the upper left-hand quadrant with the entertainers.

As audience members, we love communicators who are in the upper left. We love to be entertained! Entertainers touch our emotions; they surprise us; they make us laugh; they bring us to tears. Typically, though, they specialize in self-centered content. Entertainers hold our attention and give us a couple of hours of pleasure and delight, but generally, they are not trying to inspire us or move us to action. The self-centered content of their messages is designed to focus attention on *them* and on their performances—not on the needs and wants of their listeners.

Actors, stand-up comics, talk show hosts, musicians, and other entertainers operate primarily in the upper left-hand quadrant. Think of any ESPN SportsCenter commentator, radio personality Howard Stern, TV host Ryan Seacrest, or *The Tonight Show* host Jimmy Fallon (see Figure 3-2). In your everyday life, think of the person in your circle of friends who always tells the most outrageous stories or a great emcee at a business luncheon or awards banquet.

### Lower Right: Direct

As a result of classic leadership training, many successful and high-powered leaders fall into the lower right quadrant. Authority, rather than connection, is their MO. If you have a *low emotional connection* with your audience, yet your content is pointedly *audience-centered*, then you create an experience in the lower right-hand quadrant with the directors.

Directors don't necessarily care whether their audience trusts or connects with them; they use the License to Operate. They say, "You *will* do this, like it or not—or you'll face the consequences." They care about one thing above all: getting the job done. They value task above relationship. The audience members don't need to be emotionally engaged; they just need to comply. Audience members feel that they "have to" do what a director says, and sometimes fear is as good a motivation as any. Classic examples from this quadrant are *Vogue* editor Anna Wintour, business icon Jack "Neutron Jack" Welch, and Machiavellian military commanders (see Figure 3-2). They give an order; you have to obey. They're task-driven. In your personal life, consider your traditional boss, a commander, or a strict elementary school teacher.

### Upper Right: Inspire

Now here's a destination to which we should map much more often. To create an ideal communication experience for the audience, we must be both intentional about our message (it must be audience-centered) and intentional about the way we communicate that message (with high emotional connection).

This is the place from which we motivate, shift culture, change minds, and win supporters. Audience members feel connected and motivated to take action. These are the change agents. Who are our role models and anchors in the top right quadrant? Former U.S. presidents John F. Kennedy and Bill Clinton, civil rights activist and icon Dr. Martin Luther King Jr., former Notre Dame coach and sportscaster Lou Holtz, humanitarian Mother Theresa, rock star and humanitarian Bono, antiapartheid leader and philanthropist Nelson Mandela, and Facebook COO Sheryl Sandberg (see Figure 3-2). That's great company.

## NAVIGATING THE ROADMAP

You're probably thinking, "Get me to the upper right!" (Or at least we hope you are!) Keep this in mind: the quadrants represent the types of experiences that you create, not the type of communicator you always are. We gave you all those names and reference points, like landmarks, to help you identify the "archetypes" of each quadrant. Even on our best days, we can't produce inspiring communications all the time—and that's okay. For example, we aren't trying to inspire our dinner companions when we say, "Please pass the salt."

But each key communication situation throughout the day needs a destination. Map it! What kind of experience do you want to create? Be *intentional* about where you're going. We'll argue that there's not much of a reason to hang out in the Inform quadrant. Even if it's a quick 10-minute huddle with the team and you think the purpose is to inform, isn't there *something* you can do to make the content more relevant to your team members? Isn't there *any way* to make more of an emotional connection? Your goal is to shift your behaviors and messaging to go higher up and to the right. You will become more memorable, more effective, and more persuasive and compelling the more you create an experience that inspires.

With that larger goal in mind, let's take a look at a few examples of how being intentional can start to move you from one quadrant to another.

## Beyond Inform—
## Escaping the Bottom Left Quadrant

The parliamentary maneuver known as the filibuster was invented in 1841 by Senator John C. Calhoun and made famous by Jimmy Stewart in the 1939 movie *Mr. Smith Goes to Washington*. In 1957, Senator Strom Thurmond of South Carolina set a record of 24 hours and 18 minutes, railing against the Civil Rights Act while soothing his throat with cough drops and maintaining his strength with a steak sandwich his wife had packed for him. In September 2013, Senator Ted Cruz performed one of the goofiest filibusters in Senate history, reading a fractured version of Dr. Seuss's *Green Eggs and Ham*, doing a Darth Vader impression, quoting the reality TV show *Duck Dynasty*, and praising White Castle hamburgers—for 21 consecutive hours.

If anyone ever compares your presentation to a filibuster, we can tell you right now—that's *not* a compliment. A filibuster is long, tedious, boring, and filled with dry information. The speaker's only goal is to fill up space and chew up the clock.

Filibusterers are at the very bottom of the Inform quadrant. Few things are actually *that* bad. But they have plenty of company down there in the lower left. How many of our messages are perceived as filibusters? Time fillers? Data dumps? You can't win the people in your audience just by dumping information on them. They will resent you for boring them to tears. They will say, "This is killing my soul! This is an hour of my life I will never get back! I just want to get out of here! Somebody wake me when it's over." Being forced to sit quietly as you torture them with your information dump may actually turn those in the audience against you and your message.

One well-known business leader who is making the transition out of the bottom left quadrant is Mark Zuckerberg, founder and CEO of Facebook (Figure 3-3).

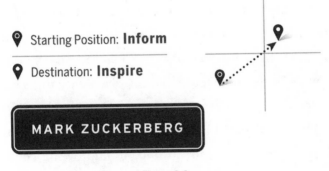

Figure 3-3

In June 2010, Zuckerberg appeared at the *Wall Street Journal*'s D8, the All Things Digital conference. There, in front of an audience, he took questions from D8's executive producers, Walt Mossberg and Kara Swisher. Zuckerberg didn't directly answer any of the questions put to him. Instead, he doggedly hewed to a few prepared talking points.

When a spokesperson comes to an interview armed with talking points, making the same tedious statements again and again and refusing to engage in a real conversation, that person is delivering an experience that's deep in the Inform quadrant. Hello, data dump! Talking points are canned information. They are designed to keep you from wandering off message and talking off the cuff. Though talking points can be useful for helping you remember your point of view and your key goals (we all forget them from time to time), they sometimes prevent you from acting like a real human being. At D8, Zuckerberg stuck to his talking points like gum on a shoe. As one conference participant tweeted, "Zuckerberg's Talking Point . . . He's said it like 99 times." (Sounds kind of like a filibuster to us!) And it wasn't exactly comfortable for him, either. John Paczkowski of All Things Digital observed that Zuckerberg was "dissolving in a lake of his own sweat" throughout the interview.[7] That's an experience that's firmly planted in the lower left of the lower left quadrant.

Immediately after his D8 communication pratfall, Zuckerberg began intentionally working to improve his communication skills. We often see wake-up calls like this with our clients, where either a bad experience, a promotion, or increased responsibility creates a tipping point for improvement.

Zuckerberg started picking a destination. Albert Costill of Search Engine Journal observed, "Zuckerberg floundered during the [D8] interview," and he noted that it was ironic that "the founder of the most well-known social media network couldn't handle sitting in front of a group of people.

Fast forward to July 2011, and . . . Zuckerberg was much better during the press conference that announced a collaboration with Skype. And his improvement was more evident on the PBS television show *Charlie Rose* in November of the same year."[8]

*Business Insider* reporter Robert Scoble, who knows Zuckerberg personally, observed, "I've seen his confidence [as a public speaker] rise, both behind the scenes and in public."[9] This confidence helped Zuckerberg get through one of the largest IPOs in Internet history, and it continues to grow and evolve now that he is leading a public company.

On an earnings call in 2013, we noted that Zuckerberg conveyed tremendous energy in his voice (a marked improvement from the monotone delivery that plagued him initially). This was no doubt an intentional move up the emotional connection axis, and inching toward Inspire. He didn't quite make it there, though—namely, because his content was still focused on Facebook's new features, "speed, stability, and the user experience," as opposed to fully linking those features to any concrete or emotional benefits for Facebook's users, analysts, and stakeholders.

There's still a lot of room for improvement. We've seen glimpses of potential—he's getting closer to the Inspire quadrant of the Communicator's Roadmap, and he is probably floating right around the point where the two axes meet. Zuckerberg is living proof that anyone can make a commitment to growth and become a more effective communicator by mapping the experience.

## Beyond Entertain—
## Escaping the Top Left Quadrant

Amy Poehler is one of the funniest women on the planet. She is a *Saturday Night Live* alum, the star of *Parks and Recreation*, and (with Tina Fey) a beloved *Golden Globes* co-host. She's an entertainer who knows how to push our laugh buttons, and she has built a brilliant entertainment career in that upper left quadrant of the Communicator's Roadmap (Figure 3-4).

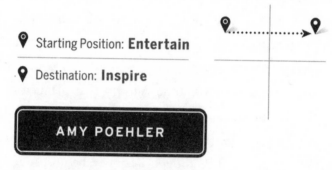

Starting Position: **Entertain**

Destination: **Inspire**

AMY POEHLER

Figure 3-4

Poehler also has a big heart for children in need, and she knows how to go beyond mere entertainment in order to advocate for the kids of the Worldwide Orphans Foundation.

In 2013, Poehler received the Variety Lifetime Impact Award, and she gave an acceptance speech at the Variety Power of Women event in Beverly Hills. Poehler invited audience members to close their eyes and think about their children and their own childhoods. "Think about the things that make you feel warm and happy and protected," she said. "Think about what made you feel okay, and what makes your children feel okay. And take that warm feeling and put it in your heart. . . . Now open your eyes and realize that there are so many children in the world who have—"

She stopped—choked—and began to cry.

"They have *nothing*," she continued, her voice breaking. "They have no one who lights up when they walk into a room. They have no clothes, no safety, no food. They have nothing. So who are we to be living this life without helping?"

The crowd applauded. Some were moved to tears themselves.

"People don't talk enough," Poehler continued, "about how good it feels to be of service. It's really selfish, but it makes you feel really good, it's good for your ego, and we should tell more people that we should do good to others because it makes us feel really good. . . . I don't want to be around people who judge or talk about what [other] people do. I want to be around people who dream and support and *do* things. And I feel I'm around those people today. . . ."

Then, to provide just the right counterbalance to the tears and inspiration, she concluded, "If you take just one thing from this event, please remember that giving to charity is good for your skin—and it makes your ass smaller."

Big laugh—and big impact.

The YouTube clip of her speech went viral. It was hardly the first time she had had a viral video. What's important here is how she was intentional about shifting from being "Entertaining Amy" to being "Inspiring Amy." Poehler mapped her destination for the experience she wanted to create. She kept all the emotional connection that she naturally has and for which she is known. Then, by shifting her content toward the right so that it was more about her audience, she moved her destination from Entertain to Inspire. It was entertainment with a purpose that inspired her audience to action.

## Beyond Direct— Escaping the Bottom Right Quadrant

The authoritarian boss, who operates in the bottom right Direct quadrant, says to the people he leads, "Do what I say—or suffer the consequences." The leader who moves up the vertical axis toward high emotional connection inspires the troops by saying, in effect, "Respond to my influence, be inspired and captivated by my vision—and your life will change dramatically for the better!"

Working for Steve Jobs was no walk in the park. A perfectionist, characterized as dismissive, hostile, relentless, and uncompromising, Jobs wanted to get things done and get them done right. According to his employees, the typical experience of Jobs was at the bottom of the vertical axis of emotional connection. "He regularly belittled people, swore at them and pressured them until they reached their breaking point. In his pursuit of greatness, he cast aside politeness and empathy, the verbal abuse never stopped."[10] He didn't do it with warmth, but boy, did he push others to action. Many people who worked closely with Jobs agree that when Jobs acted in the Direct quadrant, his pressure extracted the best from them, caused them to produce their best work, and enabled them to achieve unfathomable feats.[11]

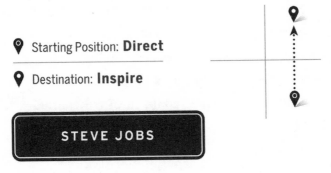

Starting Position: **Direct**

Destination: **Inspire**

STEVE JOBS

Figure 3-5

For the rest of us, the general public that got to watch him on the mainstage, his magnetic charisma and attention to detail were rock star-esque (Figure 3-5). His keynotes and announcements for new Apple products were captivating, seamless, and inspiring. Jobs was intentional about creating an experience during these mainstage events—some would even say excruciatingly meticulous. As described by Walter Isaacson in his biography,

> As always, Jobs was compulsive in preparing for the dramatic unveiling. Having stopped one rehearsal because he was angry about the CD drive tray, he stretched out the other rehearsals to make sure the show would be stellar. He repeatedly went over the climactic moment when he would walk across the stage and proclaim, "Say hello to the new iMac." He wanted the lighting to be perfect so that the translucence of the new machine would be vivid.[12]

Indeed, the experience was perfect. Couple that with the fact that his delivery came off as natural, confident, and friendly. When we saw him on the perfectly lit stage in his black turtleneck against the black screen behind him, we didn't see a slave driver, we saw an innovator.

And it wasn't without intention, work, or practice that his mainstage appearances could Inspire. Reportedly, Jobs spent two days rehearsing for each of his keynotes, working on the different segments and soliciting feedback from the product managers and engineering managers who were in the room, waiting for their turn to do a run-through. Then he would adjust his presentation for sequence and impact.[13] *That* is how he was so inspiring.

He could also map to different experiences on the fly. Remember when his clicker stopped working at MacWorld 2007? Instead of freezing (as most presenters would have done) or flying off the handle on stage (as his employees might have expected), he kept his cool and kept his high level of connection with his audience by telling a funny story about his days as a prankster in college with Steve Wozniak. He shifted from Inspire to Entertain, making for an easy transition back to Inspire.

You might be thinking, of course the master of the experience, who brought us the Genius Bar, iMac, iPhone, and iPod, was also intentional about being an extraordinary communicator. And while much has been written about whether or not it pays to be a dictatorial leader like Steve Jobs (we're not going there), what we want you to remember is how experiences are created with intention.

When you shift from Direct to Inspire, people will follow you—not for you, but for themselves. They will follow you not because they have to, but because they want to. Instead of forcing your agenda down their unwilling throats, you will inspire them to make your agenda *their* agenda, your cause *their* cause. You'll have buy-in. You'll have eager, motivated followers. You will be an inspirational, influential leader who can ignite action. This is the power of the Inspire quadrant.

## Ending Up All Over the Map

Navigating the Communicator's Roadmap isn't something you do only once. It's like working out. Just because you did an Olympic triathlon in college doesn't mean that you could do that same swim-bike-run at the same pace 15 or 30 years later, especially if you've been logging hours at your desk job instead of in the pool. You have to keep working out to stay in shape! The same is true of your communications skills—just because you have inspired in the past doesn't mean that you always will, not without working at it.

Even the most highly accomplished speakers neglect their communication skills at key moments. A prime example: President Barack Obama (Figure 3-6).

Many people consider Obama to be one of the most effective public speakers ever to occupy the Oval Office. He

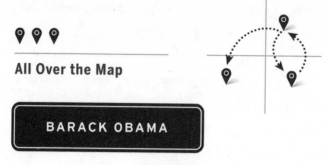

Figure 3-6

gained national attention in 2004, when he delivered the keynote address at the Democratic National Convention in Boston. One of the great moments of that speech was this:

> There is not a liberal America and a conservative America—there is the United States of America. There is not a Black America and a White America and Latino America and Asian America—there's the United States of America. . . . We are one people, all of us pledging allegiance to the stars and stripes, all of us defending the United States of America![14]

Those words, spoken in an inspiring cadence, brought everyone to their feet, stomping and cheering—and those words helped propel Obama into the White House four years later. He had it all going on: the emotional connection and the audience-centered content. He mapped the experience to Inspire, and America knew it had met a rising political star.

One of the most talked-about phenomena of both the 2008 and 2012 Obama campaigns was the "swoon effect," when people frequently fainted during his speeches. For example, at a North Carolina auto plant, he stopped speaking and said, "Looks like somebody might've fainted up here. Have we got EMS? Somebody? . . . Don't worry about it. Folks do this all the time in my meetings. . . . They'll be okay, just give 'em a little room."[15]

Now, we're not saying that Obama's impact as a public speaker actually caused people to faint—but no similar pattern of swooning has happened in American politics recently . . . maybe ever. You'd think he was one of the Beatles.

But he has not consistently maintained *that* evocative level of communication. Over the course of his presidency, Obama has been all over the map. Like many public figures, he often defaults to using the teleprompter. When he is reading his speeches in a rote, singsong manner (surprising, given his gift for oratory), he drops right back into either the Inform or the Direct quadrant. Now, admittedly, a president doesn't need to inspire at all times. After all, one of his roles is to be commander in chief. During a crisis, for example, the president can simply issue an order. Communicating from the lower right-hand quadrant—directing—is what the situation (and his job) often requires. It's perfectly all right.

But in other instances, Obama has missed some significant opportunities to influence and inspire his audiences. Case in point: the first presidential debate versus Mitt Romney in 2012. In that first of three debates, Obama remained completely in the lower left Inform quadrant. He didn't map the destination, and he made no effort to inspire his audience or create an emotional connection with his TV viewers. In fact, many media outlets used the same word, *professorial*, over and over and over again to describe Obama's debate performance.

The *Huffington Post* noted that Obama "failed to respond effectively, drifting into his professorial demeanor." The *Los Angeles Times* also called his performance "professorial, as if he were merely engaged in a ponderous academic discussion." The *New York Times* agreed that "President Obama may have sounded a bit too professorial." Reuters found Obama "professorial and a bit long-winded."[16]

After Obama's uninspiring performance in the first debate, many political pundits began writing his political obituary. Some questioned whether he really wanted to win reelection. His opponent surged in the polls. That's what can happen when a communicator creates an experience in the Inform quadrant of the Communicator's Roadmap—especially when the audience is expecting more, and the competition is delivering it. Fortunately for Obama, he had a wake-up call. He vaulted back to create Inspire experiences in the next two debates—and the rest is history.

Until it gets personal. On Friday night, February 7, 2014, our family gathered to watch the Olympics on NBC, including a satellite interview between NBC's Bob Costas, on location in Sochi, Russia, and President Obama. Our oldest son, Jackson, was nine at the time. He listened intently for three or four minutes as Obama explained why he would not personally attend the Winter Olympics in Sochi. Then Jackson turned to us and said, "Doesn't he know that everyone is watching him? Why is he doing all of those ums and uhs?"

Jackson was right (we're so proud). Even a child could see that this is not the way to communicate if you want to connect with your audience. Obama missed the opportunity to leverage the patriotism surrounding the Winter Olympic Games into support, inspiration, and influence.

Barack Obama is an amazingly inspiring speaker—when he wants to be. On the whole, however, he is all over the map.

## Within Reach

Even though our communication doesn't relate to national security or a VIP seat at the Olympics, we are all communicators in every arena of our lives. Yes, we can probably get by with merely entertaining or informing or directing others—but why settle for so little? That upper right-hand communication quadrant—the quadrant of inspiration—is within your reach.

It will feel risky to shift from creating one kind of experience to creating another. But trust us, the reward is worth the risk. The response you get will start shifting many things. Don't just take our word for it. We've been consulting and coaching with the Charles Schwab investment firm at all levels, especially with the company's top leadership cadre (including Chuck himself). Charles Schwab's chief administrative officer, Jay Allen, described the shift to Inspire as "a self-propelling engine, and once you get a taste of it, it makes you want more." It's true. Your success will become your motivation for even greater success.

In every interaction, you'll ask yourself, "Is there something I can do to increase my connection with this person?"

Instead of simply saying, "Have this report on my desk by the end of the day tomorrow," you'll ask yourself, "Is there some way I can connect with this person—some way to get this person fired up and enthusiastic about producing this report?"

We'll keep referring to the Communicator's Roadmap. Let it guide you from where you are to where you want to be. In the next few chapters, we'll show you how.

---

## EXERCISES

**WATCH**

- Notice where people fall on the Communicator's Roadmap: executives, colleagues, clients, community partners, or groups at church.

---

**THINK**

- The next time you have dinner out, don't just focus on the food. How did the host and the wait staff make you feel?

- Think about a recent experience when someone was trying to sell you something. Was it all about him? Or did he make it about you? How did it affect your response?

---

**DO**

- Map your experience of presenters at your next conference, industry event, or company kickoff.

---

### CHAPTER 4

# Behavior Reigns

*What you do speaks so loudly that*
*I cannot hear what you say.*

—RALPH WALDO EMERSON

Our family loves cooking shows—particularly the competitive ones, such as *The Next Food Network Star*. Our boys love it because of the big personalities and the crazy competitions. We love it because of Bob Tuschman.

Tuschman is general manager and senior vice president of Food Network. When he joined Food Network in 1998, it was "a low-budget cooking show channel" with "anemic-looking" programs. A year later, he was promoted to vice president for programming and production, responsible for all things programming: the development, production, and scheduling of Food Network shows, which can be seen by nearly 100 million households. Tuschman's specialty is recognizing and developing top-drawer talent; the list of stars he has brought to Food Network includes Rachael Ray, Guy Fieri, Giada De Laurentiis, and Ina Garten. Under his leadership, Food Network has become a top 10 cable network, growing in stature, audience, and profitability.[1]

One of Tuschman's most successful creations is *The Next Food Network Star*, a kind of *American Idol* for foodies. Fifteen chefs compete for the chance to land a starring gig on their own Food Network show. The hopefuls are mentored by Food Network celebrity chefs, such as Bobby Flay, Giada De Laurentiis, and Alton Brown. Tuschman and fellow Food Network exec Susie Fogelson join them on a panel of judges to evaluate the contestants.

What does Tuschman look for in a Food Network star? Obviously, contestants must be able to cook, but there are a whole lot of chefs who have the culinary chops and creativity to create a memorable dish. The real challenge is finding a great chef who can cook while being charming, engaging, and compelling . . . on camera. That takes *connection*.

Tuschman says the key to that connection is authenticity and warmth—after all, viewers are inviting that person into their homes. "I'm looking for comfort in their own skin," he says. "When you're trying [to emulate] everybody outside of yourself, you're not presenting an authentic, grounded, forceful version of yourself. What we're looking for, in a way, is somebody who has . . . a strong sense of who they are and what they want to be."[2] Tuschman continues, "There are always a few who have a natural charisma and bigger-than-life energy that instantly catch my eye. They usually become not just my favorite, but viewer favorites."

How does this translate to your communication experience? Being competent in your field is a given. No one is going to hire you, promote you, trust you, or believe in you without it. But behavior reigns. To move up the vertical axis on the Communicator's Roadmap, we need to add warmth to the equation by achieving that emotional connection through behavior.

Here's the problem: our default practice is to emphasize competence. "Here's why I'm the one for the job"; "I can tackle that challenge"; "I'll take the lead"; "I have the experience." We believe that we're confident, credible experts, and we want others to see what we see. Social psychologist and Harvard Business School professor Amy Cuddy concurs, noting that most of us in the leadership world feel compelled to prove our *competence* to other people, thinking that if we appear competent, people will trust us. That's important, but, as you'll see, research shows that we need to connect *first*.

Cuddy talks about demonstrating "warmth" and building connection and trust through communication behavior:

> A growing body of research suggests that the way to influence—and to lead—is to begin with warmth. Warmth is the conduit of influence: It facilitates trust and the communication and absorption of ideas. Even a few small nonverbal signals—a nod, a

smile, an open gesture—can show people that you're pleased to be in their company and attentive to their concerns. Prioritizing warmth helps you connect immediately with those around you, demonstrating that you hear them, understand them, and can be trusted by them.[3]

It's not our competence but our warmth, humility, genuineness, and generosity that people pick up on first when they are evaluating us. These are the qualities that engender trust and will move you right on up the Emotional Connection axis (Figure 4-1).

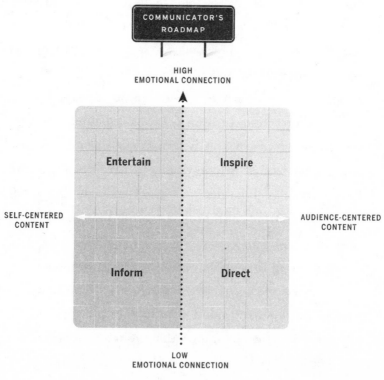

Figure 4-1

# THE BEHAVIORS OF TRUST

In 36 years of coaching and training hundreds of thousands of people, we have found that there are five key behaviors that we call the Behaviors of Trust (Figure 4-2). We'll demonstrate why the visual element (how you show up in front of others) is so profound in generating trust. We'll explain how you can use these behaviors to increase your emotional connection.

### BEHAVIORS OF TRUST

| | |
|---|---|
| **Make the Connection:** | Eye communication |
| **Keep Them Tuned In with Energy:** | Posture and movement<br>Gestures and facial expression<br>Voice and vocal variety |
| **Boost Credibility:** | Pausing |

Figure 4-2

## The Power of the Visual

Countless studies have affirmed the overwhelming power of the visual component of our senses over all others in our perception. One of the most important—and classic—studies relating to communication remains the 1967 work of UCLA psychology researcher Albert Mehrabian, who found that face-to-face communication consists of three components—what we call the Three Vs:

- Verbal (your content: the words you say)

- Vocal (tone and sound of voice)

- Visual (nonverbal behavior, such as facial expression, gestures, movement, and so forth)

Mehrabian concluded that the more the Three Vs are in agreement (congruence), the more credible and persuasive the message will be. He also concluded that when there is *no* congruence—when the words you say don't match how you come across as you say them—listeners tend to give far more weight to the visual and vocal than they do to the verbal. Figure 4-3 shows how the numbers shake out.[4]

### THE THREE Vs OF COMMUNICATION

| | | |
|---|---|---|
| **Verbal.** The message itself: | | 7 % |
| **Vocal.** The sound of your voice: | + | 38 % |
| **Visual.** What people see of you: | + | 55 % |
| | | 100 % |

Figure 4-3

This means that when people listen to you speak, they are deciding whether or not to trust you, whether or not they like you, and whether or not they believe you. If there is congruence and agreement among the verbal, vocal, and visual content of your communication, your listeners will be more likely to trust you, like you, and believe what you say. But if there is inconsistency between your words and your behavior, then people will believe your behavior and discount your words. It's as if you never said the words. The vocal and visual aspects completely block the verbal. In fact, the visual component becomes so dominant that it can flip your verbal message on its head.

Let's say you're a defendant in a court trial. You raise your right hand and say, "I swear to tell the truth, the whole truth, and nothing but the truth"—yet throughout your testimony, your tone of voice sounds hesitant and shaky, you nervously drum your fingers and avoid eye contact, and you keep fidgeting and swallowing. Don't expect the verdict to go your way. Your promise to tell the truth has been undermined by your behavior.

Now, the people in that jury box are not *consciously* comparing your verbal, vocal, and visual messages. They are forming a judgment in the blink of an eye. Do they like you or not? Do they find you believable and persuasive? They are not even consciously aware that they are forming such judgments—it's happening too quickly.

People form these unconscious judgments through a process that psychologists call "thin-slicing." This term was coined in 1992 by researchers Nalini Ambady and Robert Rosenthal in a paper in the *Psychological Bulletin*, and it was popularized by Malcolm Gladwell in his book *Blink*. Thin-slicing is the process of forming impressions, judgments, and conclusions based on a very narrow "slice" of experience. We regularly thin-slice (base conclusions on limited information) to prevent information overload or "the paralysis of analysis." It's an instinctive ability we use to read a person's facial expression and form judgments about the emotions that person is feeling. Malcolm Gladwell explains:

> Thin-slicing is not an exotic gift. It is a central part of what it means to be human. We thin-slice whenever we meet a new person or have to make sense of something quickly or encounter a novel situation. We thin-slice because we have to, and we come to rely on that ability because there are . . . lots of situations where careful attention to the details of a very thin slice, even for no more than a second or two, can tell us an awful lot.[5]

We all judge, and we do it quickly. People form impressions of you *every* time you speak. They are thin-slicing you, forming instantaneous judgments—*and these initial impressions matter*, even to those who know you well. If you want to build trust, if you want to be persuasive, then all three Vs—the verbal, vocal, and visual components of your message—must be in harmony.

One of our clients is a company that provides expert witnesses for court cases, staffed largely by scientists and engineers in various fields where more than 70 percent of the personnel have at least one PhD from schools like MIT and Caltech. These experts are often called to testify on behalf of automakers and other industrial companies, even government agencies. Our job is to help these scientists and engineers learn how to make an emotional connection with their listeners so that they will be more effective expert witnesses. It's hard for these data-driven types to accept the need for an emotional connection. "All we have to do is state the facts," they say, "and the jury will analyze the case logically."

Research shows otherwise. A 2003 study of jurors' evaluations of expert witnesses by Sanja Kutnjak Ivković and Valerie P. Hans found that jurors tend to base their verdict on an expert witness's *behavior*, not just facts and logic.[6]

Several jurors said that, when confronted with conflicting testimony from opposing expert witnesses, they relied on observation of a witness's body language, gestures, facial expression, and eyes to determine which witness they trusted. Here is one exchange between a juror and an interviewer:

> **Interviewer:** "[How did] you try to figure out, when you had the two [expert witnesses] that disputed each other, which one was right?"
>
> **Juror:** "You can tell when they lie."
>
> **Interviewer:** "You can tell? How do you tell?"
>
> **Juror:** "I don't know. If you look at people and study people, there's something you can find out, you know. . . ."
>
> **Interviewer:** "Do you look for anything in the way they speak, or is it more what they say?"

**Juror:** "You look for the way they speak. You look for the eyes. You look for the movements. . . . If he rocks like this and the other lawyer asks him a question, and he'll make like he don't understand the question. Then they're wishy-washy."

The researchers concluded, "Both the characteristics of the expert (the 'messenger') and the substantive and stylistic aspects of the testimony itself (the 'message') contribute significantly to the overall impact of expert testimony on jurors. . . . Jurors' assessments appeared to be influenced by how experts presented their information. . . . It seems that the best expert witness comes across as a very good teacher—someone who knows how to make a presentation."[7]

Whether we like it or not, even in a court of law, people buy on emotion and justify it with fact. Every time you communicate, you must have a consistent message—your verbal, vocal, and visual channels must agree in order for you to be trusted. Once people make an emotion-based decision to trust you, they will listen to your facts, information, and logic. But if they don't trust you on an emotional level, your verbal channel won't get through. Your listeners will tune you out; you might as well be talking to a brick wall. It all comes down to the consistency (or inconsistency) of your message. The words you say must be consistent with how you come across. Remember, you're creating an *experience*.

Now for the sobering part: consider the Three Vs, and now think about how much time you spend on each in preparation for a meeting, pitch, or presentation. Going back to White Lie #1 from Chapter 1, if you're like the majority of people we work with, it's close to 99 percent on verbal. We think that if we say the words, people will get it. But the message comes through us. And if that message is inconsistent, we've wasted a whole lot of time preparing content that ultimately doesn't get through.

We need to stop and ask ourselves, "How do I come across when I speak? How am I perceived by my listeners? Am I connecting? Do they trust me? Do they find me believable? Am I projecting warmth and competence? Am I creating an inviting communication experience for my listeners?"

OK, before we proceed, let's do a quick check-in. To establish an emotional connection and move our way up the vertical axis on the Communicator's Roadmap:

1. We must have both warmth and competence, and we need to bring warmth to the forefront.

2. We must have a consistent message so that the words we say match our behaviors.

Let's dive in and put the five Behaviors of Trust (Figure 4-2) into practice.

Ultimately, our behaviors are habits. The bad news is that habits are unconscious (we don't even think about them), so they're pretty hard to change. The good news is that we *can* change them! We just need to continuously push ourselves outside our comfort zones. As we move through each of the five behaviors, think of what your habits are and one thing you can start doing differently tomorrow.

## Make the Connection: Eye Communication

Consider three scenarios:

1. A cocktail party: You run into an acquaintance you are excited to catch up with, and she seems genuinely excited, too. The two of you begin a conversation, but a couple of minutes in, as you're updating her on your latest adventure, she briefly glances over your shoulder. No big deal. You continue without breaking your stride. Then she does it again. This time, you turn to look behind you to see what all the fuss is about. Oy, she's embarrassed. She noticed that *you* noticed that she was looking for someone else. Now you have no idea what you were talking about in the first place. The only hope is for a server to come rescue both of you with a canapé.

2. Your manager's office: You give a polite warning knock before walking in—after all, there's an open door policy. You notice quickly that he's madly typing away on his laptop, but before you can say, "I'll come back later," he waves you in and asks, "What's up?" The typing never ceases, and he mutters something like, "Go ahead. I'm just wrapping this up." You tentatively begin walking him through the outline

for the QBR next week, for which you really need his input, but you get only a few grunts in response.

3. The kitchen: You're talking to your significant other about plans for the weekend. He seems interested, but just when you start working through the logistics of whether or not you can actually make it all happen, he pulls his phone out of his pocket and starts responding to the latest text message, while saying "uh-huh" to who knows what. You wait in silence for him to finish.

(It should be noted that these are hypothetical situations that may or may not have been inspired by the experiences of the married couple writing this book.)

News flash: when you don't have eye communication in an in-person experience, you flat-out *don't* have communication. You have effectively lost the connection that you established.

We all have habits concerning eye communication. It's time to figure out what your habits are. Are you even making eye contact? Is it strong enough, or are your eyes darting from person to person? How might you be breaking the connection? Do you look up to think, or do you gather your thoughts while glancing down at the floor or the table? Are you connecting with each individual around a conference room table, or is your attention solely focused on the decision maker?

These eye communication habits affect the way that others perceive our warmth. Without it, we can come across as disinterested, even dismissive and aloof. Comedian Jerry Seinfeld poked fun at the device distraction habit, saying, "Do we even know what rudeness is anymore? Can I just pick up a magazine, put it in front of your face, and read it while you're talking? Is that OK?"

Perhaps more detrimental, it can also crush others' perception of our competence. One of our clients, sales training executive Lisa Contini, realized that she used to drop or close her eyes during conversations at work. "I was pausing to formulate what I wanted to say, but it came across as if I didn't know what to say," Lisa said. When she looked down to compose her thoughts during a disagreement with a colleague in a meeting several years ago, the colleague assumed that she lacked confidence and hammered away even harder, Lisa said.

Eye communication is the number one behavioral skill because it either makes or breaks our connection with our audience. Biologically, the visual sense is our dominant sense. The nerve pathways connecting the eye to the brain are *25 times thicker* than the nerve pathways connecting the ear to the brain. Of all the sensory information that our brains register, visual information has the greatest impact and makes the deepest impression in our memories. That's why eye communication is so vital to the communication experience.[8]

And notice that we said eye *communication*, not eye contact. Most people we work with are pretty good at eye contact— sure, there are plenty who look at their shoes, but for the most part, we are comfortable looking at people. The problem is that eye *contact* is not enough; you need eye communication. Looking at a colleague when you're speaking conveys confidence and respect. As the *Wall Street Journal* reports,

> Prolonged eye contact during a debate or disagreement can signal you're standing your ground. It also points to your place on the food chain: People who are high-status tend to look longer at people they're talking to, compared with others, says a 2009 research review in Image and Vision Computing. You can make eye contact with nothing more than a glance.[9]

We're pretty good at extended eye communication in one-on-one conversations. We'll typically look at the other person for 7 to 10 seconds, break for a moment to look out the window or down at the materials in front of us, and then lock back in. This feels normal, and this is the rule we recommend for conversations with one other person.

But everything changes as soon as more people enter the room. We're not sure where to look, or for how long. We don't know which person to look at: the one who is nodding and smiling, or the one who has her arms crossed and a furrowed brow. We quickly begin darting our eyes from person to person, or we look down at the floor and never make a connection at all.

Any time you're speaking to more than one person, treat them as a collection of *individuals*. Imagine that you are having one-on-one conversations with each person who just happens to be seated in a group. How long should you look at each of them? Five seconds. We take the seven-to-ten-second rule for one-on-one communications and scale it back to three to five seconds in a group environment. The goal here is to mirror the one-on-one experience to gain audience connection. But—and this is important—don't spend the full seven to ten seconds looking at one person in a group setting, because that's just downright creepy.

As the room gets larger and larger, the same five-second rule applies. You simply leverage it to your advantage. This is called the *halo effect.* You may be looking at one individual, but in a room of a larger size, there are at least a dozen people around that individual who feel that you are *looking right at them.* With one steady, five-second look, you're making a connection with a dozen people or more—and the entire room becomes connected by your eye communication. Extended eye communication shows that you care. You're involving them. *Make the connection.*

### Practice

- *Master the five-second rule.* When practicing eye communication, count to five. It may feel unnatural at first, but you'll soon become comfortable with a full five seconds of eye communication. Think to yourself: there's no one else in that room to look at during those five seconds. Practice one-on-one eye communication in your everyday conversations. And when practicing a speech, draw faces on sheets of paper and position several of these faces around the room, practicing five-second eye communication with each face. When you give individuals in your audience five full seconds of eye communication, you radiate confidence. People like and trust speakers who establish good eye communication.

- *Eliminate your traps.* Set yourself up for success. Keep your phone stashed away immediately before and after meetings, close your laptop in a one-on-one meeting, remove the confidence monitors and teleprompters at a large event (or, at the very least, learn to use those tools correctly). Don't just scan the crowd and call it "eye communication," because it's not. Get comfortable with a longer look.

## Keep Them Tuned In with Energy

Remember White Lie 2 from Chapter 1: "When I'm on, I'm great"? We learned that the truth is, "When you're *you*, you're great. Not when you're *on*." Like the political candidates we discussed in Chapter 1, the moment we turn "on" is the moment when the life is sucked right out of us and we turn into robotic data dumpers. We assume an even-keeled, "executive" presence to emphasize our competence, and everything that is warm and connecting about us from last Saturday's back-yard barbecue completely disappears.

In doing this, we offer our audience plenty of reasons to tune out. That's not great for influence and action. All that polish needs a big dose of passion. We can show it through posture and movement, gestures and facial expressions, and voice and vocal variety to increase our warmth and our position on the vertical axis of the Communicator's Roadmap.

## Keep Them Tuned In with Energy: Posture and Movement

Ray Rothrock is a partner at Venrock, a venture capital firm known for early investments in companies like Apple, Intel, and DoubleClick. Ray has heard hundreds, if not thousands, of pitches from entrepreneurs who are attempting to get funding from Venrock. He shared, "If I had to recall all the pitches that have been given to me, I'd be willing to bet that the ones who stood up rather than sat down to present either received more funding, or at least dramatically improved their chances of getting funding." By standing? Yes.

There is a huge difference in energy between standing and seated presentations. That change alone will set many of the other skills involving energy into motion. You'll move, gesture, and smile more. But just because you're standing doesn't mean you will automatically convey warmth and competence. In fact, when you lean back, rest on one hip, shift back and forth, or cross your legs in front of you, you create the opposite effect and appear less interested, or even underconfident.

Standing is good. Adding movement makes the experience that much better. In the fall of 2013, Ben attended an Association of National Advertisers (ANA) meeting in Phoenix, Arizona, where the elite of marketing and advertising come together to learn best practices and network with each other. The CMO of Walmart, Stephen Quinn, and the CMO of DaimlerChrysler, Olivier Francois, presented on the main stage and shared fascinating marketing strategies from their respective companies. They were among the many good speakers who stood behind the podium and didn't move.

Later in the day, Joseph Tripodi, CMO of Coca-Cola, began his keynote not from behind the lectern, but in the middle of the stage in front of the 1,500 or so attendees, and walked around with big gestures. He brought a whole new level of energy to the room—and it was a *big* room! Ben's first take on Tripodi was, "Confident, passionate—he owned it." The difference? Movement. He was not stuck behind a lectern. He was not pacing like a caged tiger. This was purposeful, engaging, and connecting movement. He drew the audience in.

### Use the Ready Position

The ready position comes from athletics. Picture a field full of Little Leaguers. One of our clients said that he'll never forget the ready position again because he was the coach who would yell, "Show me ready!" to the kids on the field. If baseball isn't your thing, think of the stance you would take when accepting a serve in tennis or volleyball (just don't actually crouch like you're ready to pounce—you can think that, but we don't recommend communicating this way). First, stand up straight—imagine a string pulling your head up to the ceiling—and draw your shoulder blades down your back (do not throw your shoulders back and your chest out). Then balance your weight evenly across the balls of your feet and the energy will move out toward your audience.

You can have a ready position when seated, as well. Move to the front of the seat, sit up straight, rest your arms comfortably on the table, and lean forward, without putting weight on your elbows.

### Move It!

Own your space. Movement is great, but too much movement is just as bad as staying rooted behind a lectern. Move with a purpose and then stay with a purpose. The best trick is to link your eye communication with your movement. If you're treating your audience as a collection of individuals, and you have extended eye communication, you will be drawn toward them naturally. Look at one person and walk *toward* him. Then stay in the same place and look at someone else on the same side of the room. Then look at someone on the other side.

### Practice

- *Always be ready.* The ready position is just another habit, and you can practice it anywhere. Try standing in the extended ready position with your arms resting comfortably at your sides—in the burrito line or while talking to a colleague while waiting for your triple latte. Think of that as your home base.

- *Stand up when you would normally sit down.* Energy tanks in any seated situation. As soon as you sit down, you will be more serious, gesture less, and have a softer voice. So stand! Try it in a meeting with 10 or more people.

- *Pace it out.* Own your space. Set it up to remove any barriers that would prevent movement. Walk from one side of the room to the other to understand how you can move through the space.

## Keep Them Tuned In Through Energy: Gestures and Facial Expressions

### Go Big and Go Home

Hands in pockets, hands in pockets jangling the change that's in the pockets, ring twirling, clasped hands, clapping hands, and hand washing are all nervous gestures. Nervous gestures look . . . well, nervous. These habits creep in and can distract your audience and take away from the experience you're trying to create.

Unless you come from a large Italian family like Kelly, most of us use pretty limited gestures. We make them, but they have little or no impact on the experience we create. Our elbows are glued to the sides of our body, and we gesture within a small box in front of us, safe and sound.

Gestures are another indispensable part of the communication experience. They are an excellent tool to inject energy into the equation and add a sense of ownership and control over the experience. Yet it's not easy to find that "sweet spot" between underuse and overuse when it comes to gestures. In fact, the number one question we get when coaching others on behavior is, "What do I do with my hands?"

Go big and go home. Balance between working and resting your hands. When they work, they should work *big*! Use whatever gesture you already use, then get your elbows as far away from your body as possible. Tell a fish story about how you caught a six-foot fish and show it ("It was *this* big!"). Then balance all of that with your hands resting comfortably at your sides (not clasped or tented in front of you or behind you, just comfortably at your sides).

### Practice

- *Learn your nervous gesture.* You'll need either a video of yourself or a good friend to give you some feedback. Figure out what your go-to gesture and resting position are. Then alter from there.

- *Match your gestures with your content.* If you have trouble thinking about what kind of gesture to make, try pairing a gesture with your words. For example, if you are comparing and contrasting performance from one year to the next, hold your left hand out as far to the left as possible, and your right hand out as far to the right as possible. If you have three items to cover in a meeting, raise your hand above your head and show three fingers. (*Note:* There is a limit to the number thing. We once saw a participant try to do this with the number 1,756. He raised his arm, held up one finger, then tried to hold up seven with two hands above his head, then five on one hand and back to six on two hands. A valiant effort, indeed. Only show a number up to five!)

- *Mix it up.* Don't rely on the politician gesture with your hand closed and thumb pointing out toward the audience. Don't repeat the same gesture over and over (the "server" gesture is a popular one, in which you hold both your palms up and out toward the audience as if you were holding a tray). Instead, watch other speakers and leaders. Take what works, and try it out. Expand your repertoire.

### Lighten Up

A serious face is great for poker night, when you're trying to hide everything, but it's not great for building relationships. The smile is the gatekeeper to likability. We once did a training session with the chief executive of a financial company and his senior leadership team. We noticed right away that he almost always wore a serious, unsmiling expression. We knew from talking to him that he was an upbeat, positive person—it just didn't show on his face. Time for some video feedback.

With the video camera running, we had him talk about a new initiative the company would be rolling out the following month. He talked about this plan and the great news it meant for the future of the company. Then we called his senior leadership team into the room and played back the video of his talk—but with the sound muted.

We asked, "Is he delivering good news or bad news?"

Without hesitation, everyone in the room said, "Bad news."

One person added, "From his expression, I'd say everybody is about to be fired."

Talk about an inconsistent message! The people in that room couldn't decipher the executive's verbal channel because his visual channel said nothing but doom and gloom. And he was giving good news!

Unfortunately, while this incident may sound ridiculous, it's not uncommon. A huge challenge for business leaders is showing excitement. We're taught that if we are to be taken seriously, we should be serious. After all, every decision is a multimillion-dollar decision. We loved the way an executive at a large telecom company broke it down for us: "Our corporate headquarters building is hierarchical. The execs sit on the top floor. The higher up you go in that 36-floor building, the more serious it gets."

The simplest (but not always the easiest) way to add warmth to an experience is to smile. There's plenty of research that shows that smiling, even when you don't feel like it, can be a self-fulfilling prophecy for you, and is contagious for those around you. Zen master Thich Nhat says, "Sometimes your joy is the source of your smile, but sometimes your smile can be the source of your joy."[10]

Surprisingly though, the smile also boosts others' perception of your competence. When you smile, you come across as calm, comfortable, open and warm. When you are too serious—you may be in thinking mode, during which all the other skills involving energy also become compressed and deflated—you are more closed. It's almost as if you can see the tightness, and, yes, maybe even the nervousness. When someone is smiling and open, you rarely see nervousness (whether it's there or not!).

So smile! Not ear-to-ear like a deranged maniac or a cheesy used-car salesman. Instead, think about a lightness in your face. Lift your cheeks, and open up your expression through your eyebrows. There should be just a hint of energy in your face. Get feedback from your peers on whether or not you are too smiley. The goal is to smile too much, and it's nearly impossible. In both our careers, we have seen only two people in the entire world who smile *too* much.

### Practice

- *Check your verbal and visual consistency.* Do your words match your delivery? Think of the muted video exercise described earlier. Suppose someone played a video recording of you launching an exciting new employee recognition program. If you're presenting benefits, you'd better be smiling!

- *Look for the nodders and smilers.* Those are the people in the audience who look as if they're eating up everything you say. You'll see their smiles, so smile in return. Even better, plant a friend in the audience who will smile at you and remind you to smile!

## Keep Them Tuned In Through Energy: Voice and Vocal Variety

It's undeniable that the way your voice sounds has a lot to do with the way people experience you. As reported in the *Wall Street Journal*, people who hear recordings of rough, weak, strained, or breathy voices tend to label the speakers as negative, weak, passive, or tense. People with normal voices are seen as successful, sexy, sociable, and smart.[11]

Contrast the following situations—and consider the listener experience.

First, an investor relations meeting. What are the voices you hear? Lots of monotone. Slow-paced presentations. One guy, who is a bit junior, quickly races through his slide deck. One woman, more senior, very slowly and methodically lulls you to sleep by articulating every syllable and pausing between words. Then there's the lawyer who weighs in with the painstakingly dry details, and sighs between phrases as if even *he* knows it's boring content.

Next, a barbecue with your favorite college roommates and their families. What do you hear? The sounds of catching up, patting each other on the back, and reminiscing. One guy's waving around a giant spatula as he shares the details of his last fishing trip. Another spills some juicy gossip, lowering his voice when he reveals a couple of choice "details" so that the three-year-old running around his calves doesn't start parroting those naughty words, and then all of a sudden someone pauses to announce that she is taking a two-year sabbatical to become a winemaker in Sonoma, and everybody leans in for the details.

Talk about a difference in energy! Each of these scenarios could easily be happening in your conference room, in front of your board of directors, or at a sales pitch. Wouldn't you be more engaged if that business scenario were more like the barbecue? It would certainly raise it on the vertical axis of Emotional Connection.

Next time you are communicating in a business meeting, try to imagine yourself at a barbecue. Use the same voice, personality, and vocal variety that you would use over by the grill to describe the way you feel about a new initiative. Your backyard barbecue self is the most natural, unguarded, conversational, engaging version of you. It's a reference point for authenticity.

Vocal variety is key, and you can make it work in three ways:

### Pitch

Go ahead and place monotone on that "down arrow" that anchors the vertical axis of connection. You aren't connecting with anyone if you have a flat voice.

One of the most common problems involving pitch is the "uptalker." Invisible question marks—ending sentences on a higher pitch—is a plague that has spread from middle school girls to our business communications. Maybe even to yours. We hear it a lot when executives are rattling off a list of things they want to accomplish. Most of the time, it's unconscious. They want to come off as a bit more friendly, but really, they just seem less competent.

If this is you, think about ending your sentences as statements, not questions. Try to end your sentences at a lower tone than you begin them. Think about putting a period at the end of the sentence (visually, that's down).

### Pace

It's not just the pitch of your voice but also the pace that people notice. In high-level meetings, people often think that a slooooow, steady pace is the epitome of polish. Or zapping all the excitement when you're making a recommendation. Would you talk to your family like that? No. Sometimes you can speak slowly, and sometimes you have to jamabunchofwordstogetherquickly just to Make. A. Point. This is how to tap into people's emotions and travel up the vertical axis. It keeps them engaged. Clichéd as it may be, variety is the spice of life, and it's also the goal for your pacing. Vary the pace of your voice. The sweet spot is right between too formal/ measured and too casual—it's conversational. It should feel and sound natural, as if you're at a backyard barbecue going through your key points.

### Volume

Varying the volume of your voice is the key to keeping people tuned in. If they have to lean in and listen closely to catch a key detail, you're holding their attention. But if they can't hear any details at all, you've lost them. The larger the audience and the larger the room, the greater the volume you'll need to project. The good thing is that more volume naturally increases your vocal variety and vocal range, giving you more energy and helping you connect with your audience. Just as at the barbecue, it's natural to vary the volume of your voice.

If you have a soft voice, you might *think* you're yelling. If people have trouble hearing you, focus on pushing your voice out toward your audience (not up).

### Practice

- *Diagnose yourself.* Leave yourself a voicemail or use an audio recording on your phone to listen to the sound of your voice during your next conference call or talk. Do you show passion about your ideas? Is it easy to hear the vocal variety and emotion in your voice? Are you monotone? Try to match your tone with what you feel (remember the Three Vs). Listen to see if it sounds as if you are asking questions or making statements.

- *Project your voice!* Think of pushing your voice out, instead of up (when you push your voice up, it sounds as if you're screaming at your kids, and that's not good for anyone). It's hard to slip into upspeak or a monotone pitch when you are speaking loudly. Use your core muscles and your diaphragm to help push your voice out instead of just raising your voice from your throat.

### Notes on Energy

The skills involving energy are some of the most difficult to master, because our habits are so entrenched. As you practice these skills, keep this in mind: you *will not* overdo it. We dare you to try, but it won't happen because of the disparity effect that we experience when we are changing our habits.

If you have ever taken golf lessons, you've probably experienced the disparity effect in your golf swing. The golf pro probably told you, "I want you to pull the club all the way back this far," and you probably said, "Really? Are you sure? That can't be right. It seems unnatural. It feels all wrong. But if that's what you want me to do, okay, I'll try it." And if you followed the golf pro's instructions, you probably saw a big improvement in your swing—and your game. The golf pro's instructions didn't feel right—but they upped your game. That's disparity at work. And you'll find that it works the same way in the communication game.

For example, it may feel horribly uncomfortable and unnatural to make a large gesture. While that large gesture feels insanely *huge* to you, your audience will probably say that it could stand to be even bigger, and will find you more confident, dynamic, and inspiring as a result (and you would, too, if you watched a video of yourself). Don't let comfort be your guide. In fact, if it feels uncomfortable, then you're on the right track.

As a final note, you will learn to take each skill and *dial it up and down* to make the emotional connection that's right for your audience. For example, you need *big* energy on a big stage, but you wouldn't bring that same level of energy to a one-on-one meeting. Just realize that *you* are in control of your energy, and that it is your behaviors that will communicate that to your audience, whether you are at a barbecue or giving a major corporate conference speech.

Energy is magnetizing. The more you give to your audience, the more you attract. Blend passion and polish to move up the Emotional Connection axis.

## Boost Credibility: The Power of the Pause

Consider this impressive résumé: She is an attorney and the author of seven books. She has served as the U.S. ambassador to Japan. A Radcliffe graduate, she earned her juris doctor from Columbia, worked at the Metropolitan Museum of Art in New York, and spent three years raising private funds to support New York City public schools. If she came to you for a job, would you hire her? You probably would. But not so fast.

In December 2008, this accomplished woman—Caroline Kennedy, the daughter of the late President John F. Kennedy—was being considered by Governor David Paterson for appointment to succeed Hillary Clinton as U.S. senator from New York. In fact, Caroline Kennedy was thought to be a shoo-in: She has that experience! That education! And for goodness sake, she's a Kennedy! Then she gave an interview to the *New York Times*—and the *Times* published the interview verbatim (as we have done in the Appendix).[12] Asked to explain her qualifications to be senator, she said:

> I think in many ways, you know, we want to have all kinds of different voices, you know, representing us, and I think what I bring to it is, you know, my experience as a mother, as a woman, as a lawyer, you know, I've been an education activist for the last six years here, and, you know, I've written seven books—two on the Constitution, two on American politics. So obviously, you know, we have different strengths and weaknesses.[13]

In her interview with the *New York Times*, Kennedy used the phrase "you know" a total of 142 times. Video of her interview was aired on news programs and went viral online. In spite of her excellent résumé, Caroline Kennedy did not get the job. Instead, she was panned by the public as not being able to stand the pressure; she clearly didn't have the political chops for the job. On January 22, 2009, she withdrew herself from consideration for "personal reasons."

What was it about that little phrase "you know" that cost Caroline Kennedy the appointment? She created an experience that squashed the public's perception of her competence. "You know" made her come across as shallow and inarticulate. She undermined her own credibility by the way she spoke. It's unfortunate, because it could have been avoided. A communication tragedy, to be sure.

What about you? What's your filler word of choice? Um, uh, yeah, so, well, like, literally, honestly, truly, okay? Or what about the colleague who ends every sentence with "right"? He makes one point, right? And then moves on to the next one, right? The result is the same: it undermines his message because he's asking for agreement after each sentence. The audience assumes, "He must not be that confident."

The pause is one of the most powerful behavioral tools at your disposal. The pause allows you to:

*Think.* You will lose your train of thought at some point. But give yourself a break! All you need are a couple of seconds to think, and you'll be just fine.

*Breathe.* When you talk until the end of your breath and never fully recover, your voice will start to shake, and you'll only perpetuate a vicious cycle of nerves. Pause and take a full breath in and out.

*Dramatize.* Think "Bond. (Pause.) James Bond." It just wouldn't be the same without the pause! Similarly, don't roll right over your key points. Drop a big statistic or point and pause. Let your audience think about it.

*Eliminate filler words.* Recognize your filler of choice and then use the pause to replace it.

While the pause is incredibly powerful, it's also incredibly difficult to master because it requires us to stop talking! The disparity effect here is especially pronounced. When we pause for just two seconds, it may feel like it's twice as long, and we may think the people in our audience will check out. The good news is that they experience the complete opposite effect: they don't even notice it, and they're not going anywhere.

Bonus: pausing also amps up your warmth. You are not so rushed and hurried. You are more open. It allows you to manage the cadence of your speech and convey that conversational tone. It makes you easy to listen to. Next to eye communication, pausing is the number two skill to work on for most people.

To boost your credibility, take a thoughtful moment to say . . . nothing.

### Practice

- *Try to overdo a pause.* The power of the pause has amazing impact. Just pause. Challenge yourself to resume only when the next thing out of your mouth is not a filler word but your next idea. To you, it may feel as if you are waiting for an eternity, but it won't seem long to your listeners. And over time, your confidence in the power of the pause will shorten the length of time you need to think of your next thought.

- *Plant a pause.* Get comfortable with a two- to three-second pause. Deliberately plant one in your message. Maybe it's after a story or a key point that you want your audience to remember. Once you get comfortable with using the pause, it will be much easier for you to use it when you lose your train of thought or are waiting to answer a question.

- *If you project your voice, it's really hard to say "um . . .".* That energy, pitch, and projection eliminate the tendency to add an "uh" and make you more engaging for other people who are listening.

## COMMUNICATING IS A CONTACT SPORT

You must connect to make an impact. Behavior reigns. Plain and simple.

It's the way you demonstrate warmth and competence, which helps you build trust. Your behaviors are responsible for your starting location on the vertical axis of Emotional Connection. Most of it happens before you even open your mouth. It's also one of the off-camera truths of reality TV.

*Shark Tank*, ABC's Emmy-nominated reality television series, offers budding entrepreneurs an opportunity to pitch their breakthrough business concepts, products, properties, and services to business mogul investors in the hopes of landing funding.[14] How do the Sharks, the five self-made investors, determine which contestants have the chops to get the job done?

They watch.

For five full minutes, contestants must stand facing the Sharks. In silence. And you thought pausing for two seconds felt like an eternity! Contestants are not allowed to begin their pitches until they are spoken to by the Sharks. While they are standing in front of them, the Sharks analyze their behaviors.

Here is how real estate mogul and *Shark Tank* investor Barbara Corcoran explained it:

> What I see is I see somebody who's terrible under pressure or someone who's great under pressure, and what a great test that is. Do you know before they even open their mouth, I know who I'm out on. I just sort of come up with a reason why I can say on camera, "I'm out because . . ." Okay? But the truth is I know when I'm out right away because the guy takes his hand out of his pocket, then he's shifting, he's no longer making eye contact. His eyes are going crossed, he's sweating the bullets, his knees are juggling. I mean this is a guy I'm going to give my

money to. Is he going to make it to the finish line? I don't think so.[15]

This is why we must begin by focusing on our behavioral skills! Make the connection, keep them tuned in with energy, and then boost your credibility. And be consistent.

It all comes down to this: *we buy on emotion, and justify it with facts.*

When you demonstrate warmth and competence, you are well on your way to getting buy-in—whether you're giving a big funding pitch, making a plea for a deadline extension, sharing a new vision or initiative that you are rolling out, running crisis control, selling a new product, or getting your kids to focus on their homework.

Actually, you're halfway there. We haven't even gotten to content yet.

Are you ready?

## EXERCISES

**WATCH**

- Look for consistent messages versus inconsistent messages. Note when the words that someone says conflict with how he comes across.

- Here's a justification for watching reality TV show competitions (where the prize is associated with emotional connection): How does likability trump expertise?

**THINK**

- When you meet someone new (on a project team or in an interview), what do you notice first, warmth or competence?

**DO**

- Pick two Behaviors of Trust on which you would like to work. Try to overdo those in your next meeting. For example, if you need to work on your voice, project more than you think you need to to get outside your comfort zone.

- Record yourself on video this month. Observe the two behaviors that you selected.

### CHAPTER 5

# Strike a Chord

*The one thing that you have that nobody else has is you.*
*Your voice, your mind, your story.*

—Neil Gaiman

You will rise on the vertical axis of Emotional Connection by sharing warmth and competence (through your behaviors). But there is another way for you to increase your emotional connection to your audience: through the way you liven up your content.

This is good news for all of you leaders out there who are low on the vertical axis in terms of the behavioral skills alone. Of course, it's best when you pair these two elements: behavior and content.

Jill Bolte Taylor is a great example.

You might not expect a neuroanatomist—a brain scientist—to be a riveting public speaker. But there is a reason that Jill Bolte Taylor's talk, "My Stroke of Insight," delivered at TED2008, is one of the most popular TED Talks of all time, with more than 15.5 million views. She opens her talk with the story of her brother and his struggle with schizophrenia. It was his mental illness that inspired her to become a neuroanatomist. *It's here that she opens that emotional connection with the audience and shows vulnerability rather than laser-pointing to a series of anatomical diagrams.*

Next, she explains what we know about the brain and its workings—the differences between the right and left hemispheres of the brain and how these two halves of our brains work together to make us a whole human being. *Okay, interesting, and science-y. Kind of what we expected from a neuroanatomist.*

Finally, she closes with her own personal story. She tells how, on a December morning in 1996, "a blood vessel exploded in the left half of my brain. And in the course of four hours, I watched my brain completely deteriorate in its ability to process all information. On the morning of the hemorrhage, I could not walk, talk, read, write, or recall any of my life. I essentially became an infant in a woman's body." *Audience Reaction: Jaws down, eyes wide. Emotional Connection: Fear, empathy, sympathy, disbelief.*

She describes her reaction to her catastrophic brain event: "I realized, 'Oh my gosh! I'm having a stroke! I'm having a stroke!' The next thing my brain says to me is, 'Wow! This is so cool! How many brain scientists have the opportunity to study their own brain from the inside out?'"[1]

It's a harrowing story: sometimes scary, sometimes sad, and sometimes even laugh-out-loud funny. In the course of her 18-minute TED Talk, Jill Bolte Taylor manages to wring almost every conceivable human emotion from her audience as she recounts what she learned during her eight-year recovery from that stroke. It's a great example of how to create a powerful communication experience by connecting with emotion. You'll feel why she is at the top of the vertical axis of Emotional Connection, and you'll *never* forget Jill Bolte Taylor and her stroke of insight.

She exposed her innermost suffering and her full medical history to us. Talk about vulnerability! She took a personal risk to make a point about trust. And the risk paid off brilliantly.

## EMOTIONAL CONNECTION THROUGH SHARPs

People crave emotional experiences. Logic makes us think, but a well-told story makes us feel—and emotions prompt us to action. As we learned from the Communicator's Roadmap, the goal of a communication experience is not merely to dispense information, but to engage people's emotions and move them to action. That's how we Inspire. To really cut to the emotional core of your listeners, you have to get to their memories. So it's important, as you are planning the content of your presentation, that you intentionally and strategically use emotion-triggering elements that we call SHARPs (Figure 5-1).

### SHARPs

- ▸ **S**tories
- ▸ **H**umor
- ▸ **A**nalogies
- ▸ **R**eferences
- ▸ **P**ictures and visuals

Figure 5-1

You don't necessarily need to include all five of these SHARPs in every presentation, conversation, or communication. But SHARPs are essential to creating an emotional connection between you and your listeners. If you want to drive action—close the deal, secure your budget, fire up your team—you need to appeal to people's emotions, which is exactly what SHARPs do.

Remember that deluge of information we discussed in Chapter 2? Since we are bombarded with so many messages and pieces of information on a daily basis, it's impossible for us to remember it all. SHARPs reach us at an emotional level; they help to press the brain's "record button" so that our listeners remember the most important parts of our presentation. Emotions have a strong impact on memory. That's why most of us can vividly recall both happy and traumatic events of the past—the birth of a child, the death of a loved one—even when we can't remember what we had for dinner last night. We often remember stories that we heard years and even decades earlier because SHARPs affect us at a deep emotional level.

## Stories—The Most Bang for Your Buck

In terms of the vertical axis of Emotional Connection, stories give you the most bang for your buck. NBA executive Pat Williams, the founder of the Orlando Magic, has delivered an average of more than a hundred speeches a year throughout his professional career. "Everybody loves a good story," he told us. "If I ever feel the need to wake up an audience, I know exactly what to say: 'Let me tell you a story.' Instantly, everyone in the room snaps to attention."

Stories are emotional. They stir up feelings within us—suspense, sorrow, compassion, anger, joy, and hilarity. Stories are visual. As we tell them, the listener's imagination recreates our narrative as a series of images, like a movie that plays in the mind. The vivid emotions and sensations make your listener more receptive to your message. That's why stories enable us to connect with our audience in a way that statistics, graphs, and bullet points do not. Stories move listeners to action.

David Lubars is the worldwide chief creative officer of BBDO and part of the team that created the award-winning Guinness ad featuring a brutal but friendly game of wheelchair basketball. Six guys go to battle on the court, and the spot ends with a twist: all but one of the men stand up from their wheelchairs. The friends then head to a local pub, and celebrate dedication and loyalty (with a Guinness, of course). Lubars spoke about the power of story in creating the ad. It was "a story you could see yourself in. People pass around what they believe in."[2]

You don't have to be David Lubars or Mark Twain to tell a great story, and you don't need to have miraculously survived a life-threatening situation to elicit emotion. Chances are you tell stories all the time—at work, at home, and in your community. From answering, "How'd it go at the client site?" to revealing, "You'll never believe what my daughter did this morning," to recounting, "The craziest thing happened to me as I was leaving the gym yesterday," you have tons of stories. So tell 'em.

Thanks to Andrew Stanton,[3] the creator and master storyteller of *Finding Nemo*, *Toy Story*, and *Wall-E*, here are the top four rules to live by for storytelling.

### 1. Begin with the End in Mind.

*"Storytelling is joke telling. It's knowing your punch line, your ending. Knowing that everything you're saying from the first sentence to the last is leading to a singular goal."*

When you have the end in mind—when you know what point you're trying to make—you can think of a dozen stories that tie in and relate to your point. This past year, several of our clients were preparing commencement speeches for prestigious universities. The first question we asked them was, "What do you want to say to the Class of 2014 and their families?" And suddenly, after they realized what they wanted their main takeaways to be, they had tons of stories that related to their main point.

John Thiel, head of U.S. Wealth Management and the Private Banking and Investment Group for Merrill Lynch

Global Wealth Management, was preparing to give a commencement speech to a graduating class of his alma mater, Florida State University. He wanted to speak to the graduates about the postcollege journey. Ben and John worked through some of the content. Ben asked John to think of a story or two tied to the main point he was trying to make.

John said, "I can't think of a story. I don't have a story."

This is a common response from a busy executive. But Ben didn't let him stop there.

"It will come to you."

Once he had the end in mind, or the key point in this case, John realized that, with the focus and intentionality of looking back or thinking back through his experiences, he had a dozen examples or stories that he could share that were tied to that specific point. It was now a matter of choosing the ones that would resonate most with the 1,500 graduating 22-year-olds.

Here's the question: When was the last time you built your presentation, meeting agenda, or sales pitch with the end in mind? Did you preplan the one thing you wanted to leave the audience with?

### 2. Heed the Greatest Story Commandment.

*"Make me care."*

How can you get people to care so much about your message that they'll take the action that you're asking for? *Hint:* It ain't through the logical argument. You have to get them to change something, to shift their priorities to your project, cause, or charity. And that means more than just sharing big stats, hoping that you'll impress them. It's not just about facts, figures, stats, and studies. Numbers alone don't stick.

A poignant example of this was at a Boys and Girls Club dinner where they took it to the next level. And by "they," we mean the high school students who were recognized as Youths of the Year. For four or five minutes, each took the stage and told his personal story. These 17- and 18-year-olds gave detailed accounts of gang violence, watching friends die right in front of them, enduring physical abuse from their own family members, even being locked in a trailer for 48 hours with a mother on a meth binge. They left such concrete images in the audience's mind that it became impossible for people *not* to do something.

Here's the best part: not one of these speeches was one of despair. There were only messages of hope, of how the human spirit, even in one so young, can rise above anything . . . with some help. The assistance came from the Boys and Girls Clubs throughout California that provided a safe haven, a mentor, a friend.

### 3. Make the Audience Work for Its Meal.

*"Don't give them four. Give them two plus two."*

As humans, we desperately try to bridge the gap between what we know and what we don't know. Stanton noted that we're wired for this. It's so automatic for many of us that we try to complete each other's sentences. Chip and Dan Heath wrote about creating a curiosity gap. Instead of just putting all your information out there, good storytelling is the well-organized absence of information. It's that absence that draws us in and makes us want to know more. Give the members of your audience some credit. They're natural problem solvers who like to deduce things and figure things out. Lead them down a path, revealing kernels as you go.

Here's a recent example. A vice president of sales enablement gave a presentation at an industry conference. He was invited to talk about how he had overhauled the organization. Rather than just laying out each step in the transformation, he began by drawing out the problems of the inefficient organization that he started with, and then stated, "But this all changed in less than 18 months." That audience wanted more.

Stanton cited a great quote from playwright William Archer: "Drama is anticipation mingled with uncertainty." Add some drama to your message by playing on what the audience does not know, and create a curiosity gap that people can't wait to fill.

### 4. Make It Personal.

*"Use what you know. Draw from it. [Capture] a truth from your experience. [Express] values that you personally feel deep down to your core."*

Using your own personal experiences will allow your passion and authenticity to shine. As listeners, we trust, believe, and follow those who are authentic.

Only two months after John McGee became the executive vice president of worldwide field operations for

Informatica, a California software development company, he spoke at the sales kickoff event to 2,000 attendees. This was his chance to share his vision for the company (and tell everyone in the audience what they would need to do) *and* share something about himself. Nobody really knew anything about him. John opened with a personal story.

He launched right in, "How many of you have kids? How many of you have teenagers? How many of you have taught those teenagers to drive? My daughter Maxine has been working on getting her driver's license. As a concerned father, of course I worry about her. I'm especially concerned that she might possibly do something dangerous, like texting while driving. So I bought Maxine a car with a manual transmission—a stick shift. That way she would always have one hand on the wheel and one hand on the stick shift, and she'd never be able to pick up her phone. Pretty good thinking, right? Father of the Year right here!

"I knew that once she got her license, I wouldn't be with her every time she got behind the wheel. I had to teach her to drive, and then I had to trust her to drive responsibly."

John cued a video. It showed Maxine driving her car around an empty parking lot. The car stalled, stuttered, and jerked. Clearly, Maxine was struggling to learn how to drive a stick shift. At one point, with a clash of gears, Maxine peeled out, and John's laugh in that moment echoed through the conference hall.

"Now, this is what I've been dealing with," John sighed. "But I knew that trust was the key to teaching my daughter how to drive. If she was going to succeed as a driver, and if I was going to succeed as a father, I was going to have to learn to trust Maxine.

"In case you've been wondering why I'm showing you my home videos, here's the point: it's about trust. We have to trust each other and work together more closely than ever before. Trust is the key to teamwork and collaboration—and trust must be earned."

After John's talk, and well into the rest of the sales kickoff event, people were abuzz with the concept of trust and how it could be applied throughout the organization. Again and again, in private conversations and breakout groups and the presentations of other speakers, people referred back to the story of John and his daughter Maxine as a metaphor for the atmosphere of trust that they needed to build.

Long after the conference was over, and throughout the year that followed, people often talked about John McGee, Maxine, and trust. They would come up to John and ask, "How is Maxine? How's her driving going? Any speeding tickets yet?" and John was happy to report that Maxine was doing just fine.

At the conference the following year, John got up in front of the sales team and said, "First, a quick Maxine update. Let me tell you, this young lady is amazing. She's doing great. She hasn't gotten a single traffic ticket, and she has mastered that manual transmission like a champ. And let me tell you something equally amazing. Here at Informatica, we've been implementing the lessons of trust. We've been building trust in each other throughout this organization, and it shows." Proud Papa = emotional connection. John's memorable story—so memorable that people still remembered it a year later—was not just meant to Entertain, it was meant to Inspire.

Stories can come from anywhere, but some of the most powerful stories are those that come from our personal experience. When you relate a personal incident, *you feel the emotions* of that experience as you retell it, and your own feelings help you convey that story in a powerful, passionate way. Hook your audience from the first sentence and hold it to the end. One great tool for doing that is to bookend your presentation with emotion-packed stories.

## Humor—the Serious Business of Laughter

One of the best ways to get your listeners on your side is to get them laughing. Why do people laugh? Often, we laugh when we discover a truth that has been expressed in an incongruous, ludicrous, absurd, or exaggerated form. Humor entertains and keeps your listeners engaged. As long as your listeners are laughing, or even smiling, you won't find them nodding off or reaching for their phones. When you provoke a smile or laughter, this visceral reaction is proof of your emotional connection (sending you higher up the vertical axis and making you more likable).

The key to humor is to take your topic seriously but take yourself lightly. Use common sense to keep it culturally appropriate, within the boundaries of good taste (not too vulgar to be considered NSFW—you know the drill) and politically correct. When humor misfires, it destroys the communication experience, breaks the emotional connection, embarrasses the speaker, and leaves the audience feeling uncomfortable.

Case in point: attorney Don West in the *State of Florida v. George Zimmerman* case, June 2013. Zimmerman was on trial for the murder of Trayvon Martin, and his attorney, West, inexplicably began his opening statement to the jury with . . . a knock-knock joke. It was probably the most ill-advised attempt at humor in the history of jurisprudence.

"Sometimes," West began, "you have to laugh to keep from crying. So, let me, at considerable risk, tell you a little joke. I know that may sound a bit weird under these circumstances. But I think you're the perfect audience."

Then he told his joke: "Knock, knock. Who's there? George Zimmerman. George Zimmerman who? All right, good; you're on the jury."

The jury sat stone-faced. The client, undoubtedly, wanted to crawl into a hole.

"Nothing?" West said. Then he made a pathetic plea for his joke: "That's funny."[4]

No, it *wasn't*. Joke humor (of which knock-knock jokes are the lowest form) usually can be counted upon to fall flat when delivered by a noncomedian. In this context—a highly publicized murder trial with a teenage victim—joke telling of any sort was clearly tasteless and offensive. To top it off, the point of West's joke was to insult the jury, since the punch line implied that a person would have to be completely clueless to end up on the jury. Insulting your audience is always a bad idea; insulting the jury is a hundred times worse.

What kind of humor almost always works? Self-deprecation. Making another person the object of your humor is always risky, because it sounds like an attack, and it makes you seem mean-spirited. But you can never go wrong by making a joke at your own expense. Self-deprecating humor makes you appear humble, good-natured, and likable.

Katy Keim is the chief marketing officer of Lithium, a Bay Area tech company. She has led several high-growth public companies, including Service Source and Intraware, and she regularly speaks at industry conferences to audiences of 500 people. At one memorable talk, the first PowerPoint slide was a photo of her driver's license.

"I have a confession," Katy deadpanned. "I lied on my driver's license."

Perfect opening! She got laughs from the shock value of that statement alone—and her listeners were intrigued to know what she lied about.

"I mean, look at me," she continued as she kicked off her heels. "How tall am I? Five-foot-nothing. And what does it say in my driver's license?"

The damning answer was on the screen behind her, in huge numbers: 5'1".

"You see?" Katy said in a distressed-sounding voice. "Five-foot-one! Who lies about being five-one?! For the sake of one little inch, I lied on my driver's license. That inch is a little lie I tell myself to make myself feel better about being short."

And then she connected her humor to her topic, going on to talk about the lies we tell ourselves about marketing on social media just to make ourselves feel better. Katy was funny, vulnerable, and memorable—those in the audience would not soon forget the little lady who lied on her driver's license. And they would not forget her point about being honest with themselves when they market their products and services on social media. Humor works to create an emotional connection with your listeners.

## Analogies—the Doorways to "Aha!"

An analogy is a comparison that reveals an underlying (and surprising) commonality between two dissimilar objects or ideas. Analogies use familiar examples to explain ideas and concepts that are less easily understood. They are concrete and matter of fact. Analogies help people get it.

Cognitive researcher Douglas R. Hofstadter goes so far as to say that "analogy is the core of cognition." Cognition is our human ability to process information, solve problems, and make decisions, and it has a lot to do with our ability to grasp analogies—our ability to recognize familiar patterns in unfamiliar concepts. The ability to understand analogies enables us to sort ideas and information into categories so that we can better understand reality. (You might remember this from taking or helping your children prep for the SAT.)

The ability to perceive analogies has increased our understanding of the world. Isaac Newton is said to have watched an apple fall from a tree and recognized an analogy to a planet falling in orbit around the sun because of the pull of gravity. Frederick Kekule dreamed of a snake swallowing its own tail and awoke with the realization that the circled snake was an analogy for the ring of carbon atoms in a benzene molecule. James Watson was walking down a spiral staircase at Oxford when he realized in a flash of intuition that the spiral staircase was an analogy for the double-helix structure of the DNA molecule.

A striking analogy can be a great way to kick off a presentation and hook your audience. A Silicon Valley technical engineer who went through one of our programs was preparing to speak to his management team about the need for a new set of technical standards in the company—not exactly an initiative that would be at the top of the team members' list. He needed them to get it instantly, and to care so much that they would shift resources to make this possible. His initial plan was to dive right into bits and bytes. After learning SHARPs, he opened with an analogy that immediately hooked the attention of his audience.

"The Great Baltimore Fire of 1904," he said, "leveled most of central Baltimore. It burned for two days, destroyed 1,500 buildings, and put 35,000 people out of work. It was a tragedy that could have been avoided. Firefighters were on hand from the neighboring communities of Washington, DC, Philadelphia, New York, and Atlantic City—but when they went to connect their fire hoses to the hydrants in the center of Baltimore, they couldn't. Their hoses didn't fit. Every city had a different type of hydrant, and those firemen had to stand by and watch the city burn because their hoses *couldn't fit*. Like Baltimore in 1904, our organization will suffer if we don't standardize our technical equipment and processes."

Of the thousands of talks we have seen every year, that analogy has stuck with us. It was a SHARP within a SHARP— a story *and* an analogy! It seemed as if everyone in the room had an "aha!" moment when they grasped the parallel between nonstandardized fire-hose couplings and nonstandardized technical specs in their own industry. Analogies have a way of turning a light on in our minds—and in this case, gaining the attention of management.

## References and Quotes— for Connection and Credibility

For those of you looking to take baby steps into this whole SHARP world, the easiest of all the SHARPs to add is a reference or a quote. A third-party reference and/or quotation helps us frame our message, and it brings our topic to life.

References are longer, usually a paragraph or two, and provide detailed support. Quotations are pithy and succinct, usually no more than a sentence or two.

References and quotes can help you vary the rhythms of your talk. Sometimes a quotation can encapsulate in a single sentence what might take a minute or two to explain in your own words. Quotations can make your listeners laugh or touch their emotions.

Used with care, good taste, and restraint, references and quotations can help you make an emotional connection with your audience while also strengthening the credibility of your message. It's OK to read them (if you want to be sure to get them right). Just be sure to pause.

## Pictures and Visuals—Aim for the Eyes

Using visuals in your message helps make your story come to life. There are many ways to connect with your audience visually: PowerPoints (and no, a bulleted list of words does not count as a visual aid), video clips, props, and even physical activity, such as dance, acrobatics, juggling, or stage magic. Visuals and pictures magnify the emotional impact of your message.

As you create visual aids for your PowerPoint presentation, remember the Three Bs: Make them *big* so that they can be seen from a distance. Make them *bold* so that they can be grasped at a glance. And keep them *basic* so that they don't distract your listeners from your presentation.

The New York City Department of Health and Mental Hygiene launched a subway ad campaign that showed soda being poured into a glass, except that by the time the soda reached the glass, it had turned into fat—globs of glistening, yellow human fat. They added blood vessels and even ice cubes. It was accompanied by the text, "Are You Pouring On the Pounds? Don't Drink Yourself Fat" (see Figure 5-2). The campaign urged New Yorkers to drink water, seltzer, and milk instead of sugary sodas. Pretty effective visual.

**ARE YOU POURING ON THE POUNDS?**

**DON'T DRINK YOURSELF FAT.**
Cut back on soda and other sugary beverages.
Go with water, seltzer or low-fat milk instead.

Department of
Health & Mental
Hygiene
Michael R. Bloomberg, Mayor
Thomas Farley, M.D., M.P.H., Commissioner

Figure 5-2      © 2009. Used with permission of the NYC Department of Health and Mental Hygiene.

Katy Keim, the 5'0" CMO who lied on her driver's license, loves SHARPs so much that she is always trying to outdo her previous SHARP. She revealed her latest claim to fame when she launched new messaging for her technology company that was so simple that *even your parents could understand it.*

In front of the Lithium sales and marketing team of 200 people, she said, "No, really. The new messaging is so simple, your parents can understand it. Let's ask my dad." Then she called *her father* on Skype. From the main stage.

"Hi, Dad!" she said.

Her 80-year-old father's face appeared on a giant screen behind her. "Hello, Katy! I see you—and I see your audience, too. Hello, everybody!" He waved.

"Dad, I want to run something by you."

"Sure, Katy, whatcha got?"

"Dad, does this make sense to you?" And then she explained the new messaging.

Their conversation was warm, funny, and touching—and persuasive. It was clear to everyone from half a continent away that even an octogenarian could, indeed, understand the new messaging.

Now, let's consider a few examples that don't need any technology in order to be effective. You can spur audience involvement by passing things out to your audience.

A presenter at Google's annual developer conference once planted red and green glow sticks under the chairs of each member of his audience. He asked them to grab them and light them, and then he conducted a poll. He asked the audience members to hold up the green glow sticks if they agreed, and to hold up the red if they disagreed. When the room lit up in unison, it was clear that they were ready to hear his latest initiative.

At VMware, a participant once began his prepared talk to a room of 10 people by holding up a big sealed brown paper bag. He said, "This bag holds a valuable commodity. What do you think it is?" He built a bit of suspense before he opened the bag and passed out "the gift of time": neon watches for every single person in the room. It was clever and unexpected, and it perfectly illustrated the benefit (of saving time). In addition, it's hard to forget the neon watch on your wrist and an easy way to spur conversation in the hallway with coworkers who didn't receive watches.

Sometimes the most effective visuals are produced from the simplest ingredients. We once attended a church service at which the pastor made a powerful point using only one simple prop.

The pastor invited a young man from the audience to come up on stage with him. The pastor handed the young man a glass of water filled to the rim. "Just hold that glass for a moment," the pastor said.

So the young man held the water glass in front of him. Meanwhile, the pastor continued to talk and gesture—and he bumped the young man's arm. Water sloshed out of the glass and splashed on the pastor. The pastor turned accusingly and said, "Why did you spill water on me?"

The young man looked chagrined. "Because you bumped me."

"I know I bumped you. But why did you spill water on me?"

"Uhh—I spilled water on you because you bumped my arm."

"Let me put it this way: Why did you spill *water* on me? Why didn't you spill coffee? Or lemonade? Or tomato juice?"

"Because that's what was in the glass—just water."

And that was the pastor's point. Every day, we are filling ourselves up with good character choices or bad character choices. And eventually, life is going to bump us and cause what's inside us to spill out. The knocks of life are going to reveal whatever is stored within us—either courage or cowardice, forgiveness or resentment, selfishness or self-control.

It's a powerful visual analogy, yet the props were so simple—just a drinking glass, water, and a participant from the audience.

## THE REAL POWER OF SHARPs

Over the years, we've heard it all: "I can't think of anything." "I'm not creative enough." "We're data-driven here at my company." "I don't buy it." "It's a 'nice to have,' but I'd rather focus on the 'need to have' parts." "This is just too risky." "It's not what we do here." "I don't have any stories." "I don't have time to research a quote."

First, many business leaders think that every aspect of their presentation must be perfect. If they don't perceive themselves to be good storytellers or good at humor or good at one of the other SHARPs, they don't even want to try it. Often, business leaders tell us, "Storytelling isn't my thing.

I'm just going to go up there with my charts and graphs and bullet points, and that'll be good enough."

The second reason business leaders often resist using SHARPs is that they think that SHARPs are fluff, unimportant entertainment elements that get in the way of the message. But SHARPs are not fluff. SHARPs make people sit up and listen. They are powerful tools that enable us to connect with other people, reach them at an emotional level, and persuade them of our point of view. SHARPs don't have to be perfect to be effective. They just need to touch our listeners' feelings and perhaps evoke a smile or an empathetic nod.

As a leader, one of the best ways that you can create an emotional connection is to be vulnerable. Sometimes you don't know what will strike a chord. You don't know which story, analogy, visual, or reference is going to connect. So you have to put a lot out there, and it can't just be data.

A big trend we are seeing with our clients is that more and more of them want to learn the right way to open up. Many of them see their personal lives and their professional lives blending more now than ever before. So what is considered vulnerable, and what is oversharing? Based on 12 years of research, Brené Brown, PhD, LMSW, describes:

> Vulnerability is based on mutuality and requires boundaries and trust. It's not oversharing, it's not purging, it's not indiscriminate disclosure, and it's not celebrity-style social media information dumps. Vulnerability is about sharing our feelings and our

experiences with people who have earned a right to hear them. Being vulnerable and open is mutual and an integral part of the trust-building process.[5]

Vulnerability is hard for leaders to achieve, but it will help your team members relate to you. Sheryl Sandberg told the Harvard Business School Class of 2012, "When you're the leader, it is really hard to get good and honest feedback, no matter how many times you ask for it. One trick I've discovered is that I try to speak really openly about the things I'm bad at, because that gives people permission to agree with me, which is a lot easier than pointing it out in the first place."[6]

Whenever you make yourself vulnerable by sharing a personal story from your own experience, especially a story in which you lay open your fears and anxieties, your weakness and insecurity, your faults and failings, you touch the emotions of your listeners in a powerful way.

Ben recalls, "I once worked with a very high-level leader at a Fortune 100 company, and I expected to be wowed by him. Instead, the leader came off as aloof and disconnected. Throughout the day that we worked together, we made very little progress. I couldn't figure out whether he was consciously resisting the training or whether he simply didn't understand how to apply it. I only knew that I was frustrated by the lack of success I was having with him.

"Then, during a panel discussion, the leader shared that his mother had died some years earlier. He spoke haltingly, but vulnerably, about how his mother's death had affected him. As he spoke, my frustration with him melted away, and I felt empathy for him. It was the first time I really *liked* him.

"Now, I know that part of the reason I warmed to him was because *my* mom had died when I was young as well. Yet his SHARP—his personal story of the loss of his mother—would have created a bond of empathy and connection with *any* listener, even one that had never lost a parent. As a speaking coach, I could have critiqued several behavioral aspects of his presentation for ways he could have added more energy and passion. But as a listener, I was riveted, I was connected, and I was won over. Authenticity and vulnerability coupled with a story—that was true leadership right there. That's the power of a story. That's the power of a SHARP."

We've learned all about creating the emotional connection. To travel north on the vertical axis, you must demonstrate the behaviors of trust, and you know how to cut deep with SHARPs in your content. Now we're going to bring these two pieces together as we move toward considering the actual core of your message and how you can shift to the right on the horizontal axis toward other-centered content.

## EXERCISES

**WATCH**

- Watch Jill Bolte Taylor's TED Talk, "My Stroke of Insight." We dare you not to be Inspired.

- Watch Andrew Stanton's TED Talk, "The Clues to a Great Story," and grasp the storytelling principles.

- Watch Brené Brown's TED Talk, "The Power of Vulnerability."

---

**THINK**

- Think about ways you can share vulnerability. What types of things have helped you connect?

- Think of a great analogy for your next initiative, or a great analogy to share your work life with your friends, family, and/or kids. Try it this week.

---

**DO**

- Keep a story journal. How did you choose your career? Who had an impact on it? Has anything interesting happened this past week or month?

---

### CHAPTER 6

# Move from Information to Influence

*What would happen if you wanted to persuade
a bunch of people to come along with you on a
journey? What are the two things you need to do?
Well, you've got to start where they are and you've got
to give them a reason to come with you.*

—CHRIS ANDERSON

Old habits die hard. Not just the ones we've been talking about concerning behavior, but also habits surrounding how we prepare our content.

In May 2013, we sat down to prepare for our annual Decker board meeting in June. What was the first thing we did to prepare? Whip out the previous year's PowerPoint deck, of course. We sat there for a good couple of hours, updating the 2012 charts and figures. Time went by, and our frustration grew—the story just wasn't coming together. And we had a good one to tell! We kept flipping back and forth between the slides, moving them from one section to another, then finally . . . we slammed the laptop shut.

What happened? We had slid right back into our old habits, and we had gone about preparing a message in precisely the way that we should not. Taking out the previous Power-Point deck? Are you kidding me? It's the cardinal sin of all message preparation. We should have known better—we teach this, after all!—but we fell into the trap ourselves, lured by the shiny structure, the completed slides. We thought, "We're overcommitted right now and don't have much time, so we'll just use last year's as a template." So sad. As our boys would say, "Epic fail."

Sound familiar? We're all under pressure, and we all have zero time, so when we're asked to create a presentation for an internal or external meeting, we head straight for whatever we've done before. The last quarter's report: I'll update the number. The last client presentation: I'll change the logo. The result is a data dump, a whole lot of PowerPoint abuse, and gobs of precious time wasted.

And it's not just a data dump for your audience; it probably feels like one for you, too. Have you ever felt totally and completely bored by your *own* message? We've had many clients come in who were disengaged from their messages. And they should be! Their approach is, "Same story. Different day." Think of wholesale insurance brokers who travel around the country selling products and services, product managers in a high-tech company conducting new product rollouts across regions, or senior leaders doing a town hall road show to launch a new initiative. They don't shift the message; they just share it—again and again and again. And they get bored doing it. Shocker.

Now put yourself in the audience. Think of the meetings and conference calls you attended in the last week. How many of those meetings were necessary? How many of those meetings were frustrating? How many times did you think, "Why am I here?" Did you leave with a clear plan? Did you think an e-mail could have sufficed to deliver the salient points? Why are so many of these meetings so bad?

We went over the white lies in Chapter 1, and most meetings fall into the category of White Lie 3: "I don't need to prep. I can wing it." Or sometimes, "I just don't have time to deal with this right now." Meetings are unfocused. Many of them are status updates, weekly reviews where you just talk and talk about what you've already done. But it feels like it is just taking time away from what you are doing. What is the point?

Well, enough.

It's time to move from information to influence. The Communicator's Roadmap points the way. We must shift along the horizontal axis from Self-Centered content to Audience-Centered content (see Figure 6-1). This is the missing coordinate that we need if we are to shift our communication to action and seize the opportunity to *change something*. Change the way people think or act about your initiative, idea, product, service, and process. Moving from information to influence will land your experience either in the Direct quadrant or, hopefully (because you're mastering the emotional connection), in the Inspire quadrant.

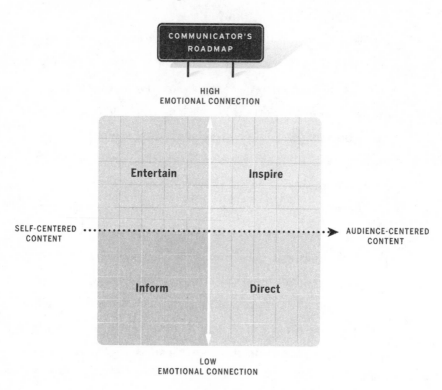

Figure 6-1

We are going to teach you a system that not only will revive all those meetings you attend and lead but will allow you to motivate change. It will also change the way you think about your voicemails, quick chats in the hallway, impromptu meetings with your boss, and opportunities to catch decision makers. Instead of thinking, "How can I impress this person?" or, "What's the checklist of items I need to bring to this meeting?" you will change your mindset to, "What is the point of this meeting? Who's going to be there?

How can I drive action? What can I do to motivate them?" You will learn to create a focused, Audience-Centered message, and you will save time doing it.

Does this sound too good to be true? It's not. You just need a framework.

The Decker Grid is a tried-and-true system that has been part of the Decker Method for 36 years. It will allow you to develop any message easily and consistently. Learn it and use it regularly, and you will:

- Dramatically reduce the time it takes to prepare a talk.

- Speak confidently in every situation, even on a moment's notice.

- Get your listeners' attention and improve their retention.

- Get to the point.

- Persuade and motivate action.

There's no need to write out speeches and then read them to a bored audience while standing rooted behind a lectern. The Decker Grid describes a very creative process that enables you to deliver a brilliantly organized yet spontaneous conversation with your listeners.

We're going to jump right in and walk you through the Decker Grid.

*Note:* The next two chapters will read like a cookbook. Our goal is to give you a step-by-step, repeatable recipe that you can use for any message. First, let's start with the ground rules and a few tools you'll need:

1. The first rule of message preparation: Plan analog and then go digital. Keep your laptop shut and grab a pen and paper (or, more specifically, a pad of sticky notes).

2. Write trigger words (one to seven words to trigger your idea) on sticky notes. Since you're never going to start thinking about what to say by opening up PowerPoint, you'll want to use the small sticky notes to write down just a few trigger words to capture your ideas (rather than crafting every perfect word). The key here is that you don't want to write a full script. As you're about to learn, a few words will help you stay focused on your main points. The advantage of sticky notes is that you can pick them up and move them around to organize your message—far better and more effective than copying and pasting sentences and points in your outline. They're as free and flexible as your ideas.

3. Find or fashion yourself a Decker Grid to follow along the process. You can head over to decker.com to download one, or create a makeshift one of your own using a manila folder or a couple of pieces of paper. It will help guide you in the process.

## Using Sticky Notes

Here's a helpful idea for using sticky notes to assemble your Cornerstones and other speaking notes: use them upside down. Make sure the tacky strip is along the bottom of the note instead of at the top. Why? Because sticky notes tend to curl away from the tacky strip. When you use them upside down, they will curl toward you and be easy for you to see instead of curling away from you.

*Note:* Please do not rewrite everything if you forgot to turn them upside down (they'll still work right side up).

# THE DECKER GRID: A SYSTEM IN SHORTHAND

Here's a quick preview of the Decker Grid to show you where we're headed. The grid (as our clients affectionately call it) is a four-step process:

1. *Cornerstones.* Focus your message.

2. *Create.* Brainstorm the supporting ideas.

3. *Cluster.* Organize your thoughts.

4. *Compose.* Edit your final message.

The Cornerstones are the most important part, and this is where we need to spend the most time. Incidentally, this is also the part of message planning to which people typically (and incorrectly) dedicate the least amount of time. We'll use the rest of this chapter to lay out the Cornerstones, and then you'll learn how to expand and complete your message in Chapter 7.

## STEP 1: THE CORNERSTONES—
## FOCUS YOUR MESSAGE

In the building trade, a cornerstone is a foundation stone. It plays a key role in the construction of a building. Once the cornerstone has been laid, all the other stones will be laid in reference to this one stone. How you lay your cornerstone determines how you will build the entire structure.

When it comes to planning a message, talk, or directive, the Cornerstones of the Decker Grid serve the same function. They help you frame your message. And by "message" we mean how you talk about everything, from big things like town halls and QBRs, to new business pitches, to weekly team meetings, to one-on-ones with your boss, and right down to your voicemails (if you are even going to leave one these days) and introductions. What are you saying? What do you want to say? The answer lies in the Cornerstones.

The Cornerstones define your audience and guide your content creation so that whatever you say is relevant and actionable. They are so important that they will determine all the key points and ways you will frame and build the rest of your talk. The Cornerstones keep you focused on what is important *to your audience,* so that your message shifts from Self-Centered content to Audience-Centered content.

The Cornerstones have four elements, each serving an important mission in framing your message (see Figure 6-2):

## 1. Cornerstones: Focus Your Thoughts

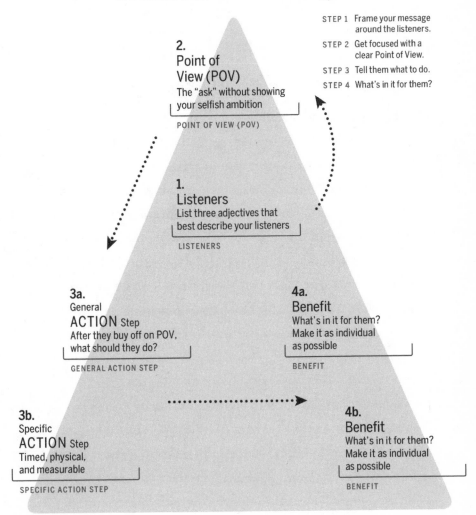

STEP 1   Frame your message around the listeners.

STEP 2   Get focused with a clear Point of View.

STEP 3   Tell them what to do.

STEP 4   What's in it for them?

**2.**
**Point of**
**View (POV)**
The "ask" without showing your selfish ambition
POINT OF VIEW (POV)

**1.**
**Listeners**
List three adjectives that best describe your listeners
LISTENERS

**3a.**
General
**ACTION** Step
After they buy off on POV, what should they do?
GENERAL ACTION STEP

**4a.**
**Benefit**
What's in it for them?
Make it as individual as possible
BENEFIT

**3b.**
Specific
**ACTION** Step
Timed, physical, and measurable
SPECIFIC ACTION STEP

**4b.**
**Benefit**
What's in it for them?
Make it as individual as possible
BENEFIT

Figure 6-2

1. *Listeners.* Make it about them.

2. *Point of View.* Find the lead of your story.

3. *Action Steps.* Make it concrete.

4. *Benefits.* Make them care.

At the center of it all is the most important component: listeners. Let's start here.

## Listeners: Make It About *Them*.

Who's listening? Your audience members want to be moved. In order to reach them, we need to get to know them and design our message to *directly* meet their interests, wants, and needs.

You may be thinking, "Thanks. Mind-blowing stuff here. *'Target your message to your audience.'* I'm pretty sure I got that in Messaging 101." You're right. It's not rocket science, and it's something you've certainly heard before. However, while it's not earth-shattering in principle, it is rare to find it in practice. We all have the best of intentions, and most of us *do* think about the audience as we're preparing what we want to say or planning the result we want. But this cosmic thing happens when we open our mouths and begin to speak: the message is transformed into *our* message, and we don't even notice it's happening!

First and foremost, in the process of influencing someone—when we're asking that person to do something— we feel compelled to prove ourselves: to prove our credentials, our competence, our capabilities, our team, our product, our process, our service, and on and on. We lay out all the reasons for our idea: why me, why us . . . and all of a sudden, it has nothing to do with *them*. It's like that old saying people use for a breakup, "It's not *you*. It's *me*." A crushing blow to a tender young heart. Well, that's exactly what we communicate. We say, "It's not you. It's *me*, and here's *everything* about *me*." This might be a good excuse to get you out of a relationship, but it's not one for you to use every day. In this case, it's a crushing blow to your audience.

What else happens? We drive our own agenda. We see this happen a lot in sales. "I want to describe my shiny new object for you." Why? Because I have to make my quota; because I need you to buy it; because I have the shiniest shiny new object in all the land. No matter what we want or hope or try to get across, we end up like Marissa Mayer at Cannes Lions. Instead of leaving her listeners to deduce for themselves that Yahoo! is the place to advertise, she shoved it down their throats to such an extent that they pushed back at her. She could have achieved so much more if she had spoon-fed little nuggets that *related to her audience,* the creative community of Cannes, instead of centering around Yahoo!

It's not just on the main stage that this happens. We'll do this anywhere. Take, for example, a sales pitch that was left on a voicemail for Kelly. She recalls, "I remember thinking, what a joke! And then right before I hit delete, I thought, 'This would make a great example of what *not* to do. I'll use it for training purposes!'"

Here's the transcript of the voicemail:

Good morning! Sorry I missed you. Ma'am, we primarily deal with speakers and consultants. What we do is, we help them achieve larger Internet exposure. We do have the National Speakers Association's top speakers as clients, and we'd like the opportunity to do the same for you. And we are cost-effective and proven to increase business and Internet exposure. We are world-class. We'd very much like to hear from you if you're interested. My number is [phone number]. We'd very much like to hear from you about what we can do to help you achieve far greater exposure. Have a great day. Buh-bye.

Anything stand out from reading the text? Let's take another look at just the first part:

Good morning! Sorry I missed you. Ma'am, *we* primarily deal with speakers and consultants. What *we* do is, *we* help them achieve larger Internet exposure. *We* do have the National Speakers Association's top speakers as clients, and *we'd* like the opportunity to do the same for you. And *we* are cost-effective and proven to increase business and Internet exposure. *We* are world-class . . ."

A count of seven *we*s and two nonsubstantive *you*s. As one of our clients noted, "It's we, we, we . . . all the way home."

You may dismiss this example as a junior salesperson dialing for dollars and reading off a script. Okay, he probably was reading off a script. But every time we create a message, we're writing a script, too! We fall into the *same* trap of feeling the need to prove our agenda and ourselves. It's not about *us*. We need to make it about *them*.

Since our goal is to influence others and to persuade them to take action, we can't talk all about ourselves. Instead, we need to step back and ask ourselves some key questions about the audience. This is a critical step in the process, even, or especially, if you know your audience well—for example, your team, your boss, or a key client. While you may have worked with these people for years, and understand how they think about and approach a situation, that doesn't mean that their same opinions, thoughts, and goals translate directly to another subject.

Take some time and think about your listeners:

- Who are they?

- Why are they here? What are they expecting from this message?

- What do they know about the subject, and how do they feel about it?

- Are they data- or business-driven? (Are they interested in facts, figures, and details or in big-picture business problems?)

- What would make them resistant? How would they challenge the message?

- How can you help them? What problem are you trying to solve that will make their life better in some way?

The answers to these questions will help you understand how to shift what you say—and then make it more relevant and/or motivating to *them*.

Once you've answered the questions about your listeners, pick the top three adjectives that describe them. For instance, resistant, open, hostile, skeptical, friendly, budget-conscious, and so on. These three words make up your Audience Profile. Keep this Audience Profile top of mind, as it will help keep you focused on *them* through the message planning process.

### Let's See It in Action

Let's go back to that voicemail sales pitch from the junior salesperson and reframe the message using the Cornerstones. In his version, the listener was pretty generic ("anyone from my list"). *Note:* You're not always going to know everything about your audience, but find out what you can; even one thing can make the difference.

We did a little digging, and we found out that his company was in the business of search engine optimization (SEO). It helps its customers move higher up on Google, Bing, Yahoo!, and other such sites. If that salesperson had simply searched for "communications training," he would

## Curse of Knowledge

One note of caution as you proceed with this exercise: beware of the Curse of Knowledge. Brilliantly addressed in *Made to Stick* by Chip and Dan Heath, the Curse of Knowledge is a devastating epidemic plaguing messages everywhere. It's a blind spot that prevents us from realizing what our audience does and does not know. We assume that just because we use acronyms like SHARPs, everyone else knows what they mean, too. Every day, we have to think about to whom we are speaking, and we have to shift what we are telling those people.

Here's a quick personal example: if I have a problem with my computer, I'm going to call IT. Keep in mind that I don't speak IT. All I want to know is what single button I can push to make the problem go away. The person at the Help Desk, however, assumes that because he speaks IT, I must also possess this talent. So he starts using terms such as gigahertz, RAM, processing speeds, bits, and bytes. Effective communication? Not so much—at least not for me, and I'm the one listening. Had this help desk specialist known that I didn't want to know *how* it worked or *why* it wasn't working, and that I am a busy executive with a big deadline who just wants to know what button to push, he would have told me to turn the machine off, wait 45 seconds, and turn it on again. Just like that. Exactly what I wanted. You can beat the Curse of Knowledge if you really think specifically and deeply about your audience members.

have found that at the time, Decker invested very little in SEO (in fact, most of our business was driven by word of mouth, and much still is). So, for this example, let's say he's now talking to a prospect with a poor search ranking. Your sticky note might look like Figure 6-3.

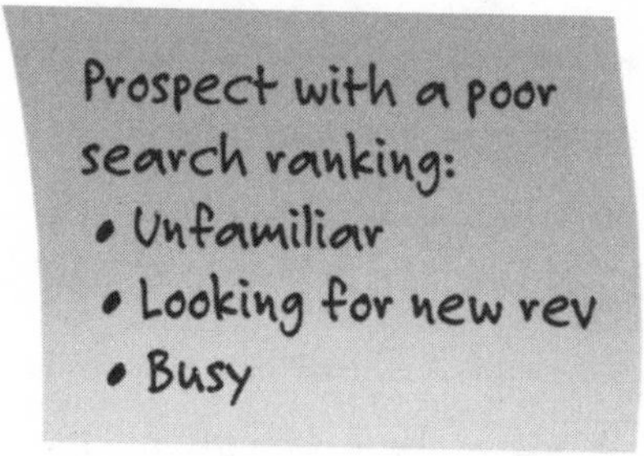

Prospect with a poor
search ranking:
• Unfamiliar
• Looking for new rev
• Busy

**AUDIENCE PROFILE: LISTENERS**

Figure 6-3

Voilà! After identifying your Audience Profile, you are ready to think about the big picture, and what approach will move that *specific* listener along the horizontal axis from information to influence.

## Point of View: Find the Lead of Your Story

Now for the tough part: you have to pick one thing to say. Really. One, and only one. You must find the lead of your story. Remember Andrew Stanton from Chapter 5: "Storytelling is joke telling. It's knowing your punch line, your ending, knowing that everything you're saying, from the first sentence to the last, is leading to a singular goal."[1] What is the one point you want *them*, your audience members, to take away? This is your Point of View.

Your Audience Profile is the perfect way to find your Point of View: Start where your listeners are, and give them a reason to come with you. That seems so simple, but it's rarely put into practice. In our executive sessions, we'll ask, "What do you want the audience to do at the end of all this?" Nearly every time, the response is a very thoughtful, and sometimes a pretty long, pause.

So what exactly is a Point of View? Think of it this way:

- Your big idea and the lead of your story; the one thing that you want everyone in the room to walk away with; the goal of your entire presentation—everything in your talk will build toward it.

- The biggest change in how you want your listeners to think about or act on your idea.

- The "ask" without showing your selfish ambition: highlighting why it's relevant to them.

Once you've determined your Point of View, write it down as the second Cornerstone of your message (see Figure 6-2).

Got it? Let's check it.

Here's what a Point of View is *not*:

1. A Point of View should never include your company or organization name or the name of a product or service. That's Self-Centered content. If you're

a salesperson, your customer already knows what company you represent and probably knows something about the product you're selling. To shift to Audience-Centered content, you need to think about what it means to *them*: How will it help *them*? What's the opportunity for *them*? Why would it be beneficial for *them* to think differently about it?

2. A Point of View is not informational. Our goal is to move to the right on the Communicator's Roadmap. Your goal is not merely to Inform but to cause *a shift in thinking* within your listeners from the beginning to the end of your talk. A Point of View is designed to persuade your listeners and *move them to action*, so you should be able to state your Point of View as a phrase or sentence that encapsulates the change you want your audience to embrace, adopt, and implement.

3. A Point of View is not about you. It's the ask *without showing your selfish ambition*. It's a common goal that we can agree on. The response you're looking for is a nodding head. You want your listeners to say, "Tell me more," rather than, "Can we go now?"

Here's an example of a Point of View that was *not* focused on the listener. One day, while Ben was working at his desk, one of our team members dropped by and asked if Ben had a few minutes. We have an open-door policy, so naturally Ben agreed. He sat down and said to Ben, "I think we're being too shortsighted." He went on to explain a fairly easy request for a new client. Unfortunately, he lost Ben with his opening statement. It was enough to knock Ben onto his heels, and he immediately took a defensive stance. Why? While the assertion might have been true, the whole idea of the Point of View is to get those in your audience to come along on the journey with you—not to stop them in their tracks.

If we could wipe the slate clean, this could have been a completely different experience. If he had gone to Ben with, "We need to ensure that a first touch with a new client goes well," Ben would have said something like, "Of course. Tell me more," and the whole conversation would have lasted two to three minutes, tops. Find the lead that matters to those in your audience. The goal is to get them on your side. Move them from information to influence, and open the door to Inspire.

## Dealing Cookies

When you shift from Self-Centered to Audience-Centered content, you can sell and influence anything—and it's an important lesson for all of us, whether we're in the corner office selling a hedge fund or in front of the grocery store selling Girl Scout cookies.

Your presentation needs a lead—a clear, succinct statement of the central idea of your message. Entrepreneur

*(continues)*

Seth Godin blogged about the importance of finding the right lead for selling Girl Scout cookies—or for selling any other product or idea.

"Teaching young people to sell," Godin writes, "is a priceless gift . . . that can pay off for a lifetime." Unfortunately, he adds, the Girl Scouts organization teaches its members to "memorize a fairly complicated spiel, one that involves introducing themselves, talking in detail about the good work that the Scouts do, and finishing with how the money raised goes for this and for that." In other words, the Girl Scouts are taught to frame their message around the organization's agenda, not the listeners' wants and needs.

Godin suggests a different approach—a message that is not only simple and easy to memorize but 100 percent listener-focused: "What's your favorite kind of Girl Scout cookie?" With this single, simple question, he adds, "the power in the transaction shifts, with the Scout going from supplicant to valued supplier." What's more, the question doesn't invite an answer of "no, thank you," but instead asks the listener to choose his favorite variety.[2]

Let's go back to the example of the voicemail sales pitch that Kelly received. The Point of View, or lead of the story, from the original voicemail was something like, "We provide greater Internet exposure." We know that wasn't very effective because it's not listener-focused. We know that the listener (in this case, Kelly) was a prospect with a poor search ranking who was unfamiliar with digital marketing and was looking for new revenue and that she was busy. The whole point of the voicemail was to try to change the way the listener (Kelly) thought or acted vis-à-vis SEO. Creating a Point of View around something called "greater Internet exposure" wasn't a good idea because it wouldn't necessarily mean much to this listener, especially since she may not even know what SEO is (a little Curse of Knowledge in action here). Nor should the salesperson have led with "Sign up for this service" because that would take him right back to the Self-Centered side of the axis.

He needed to convey the importance of adding some digital marketing to Kelly's existing efforts. He was trying to change the way she, the listener, thought and acted about SEO. Let's focus again on the listener's needs. He knew the listener was probably a small business owner who hadn't invested time or money in digital marketing but could be interested, especially if it meant a competitive edge. A better Point of View for the salesperson would have been, "Your prospects must be able to find you *first*" (see Figure 6-4). In other words, you're missing out on potential business because you have been ignoring this channel.

The opening quote of this chapter by Chris Anderson says, "You've got to start where they are and you've got to give

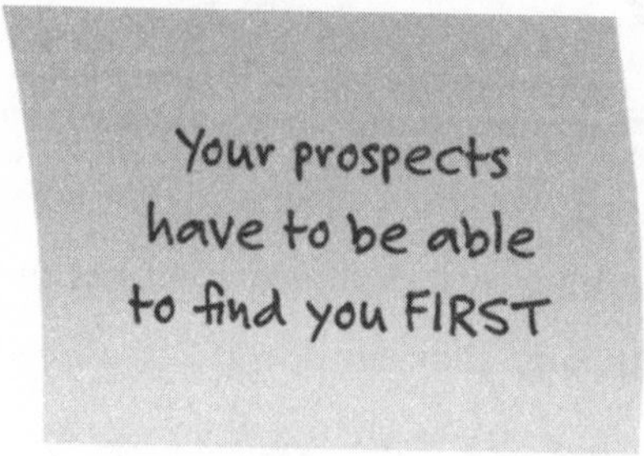

*Your prospects
have to be able
to find you FIRST*

**POINT OF VIEW (POV)**
Figure 6-4

them a reason to come with you." This Point of View does just that—and has the power to shift the listener's mindset from Inform ("thanks for the information about your company") to Influence (either Direct or Inspire): "this has the power to transform my business."

## Nail the Point of View

Netflix is often cited and lauded as the amazing innovator that disrupted the video rental industry and put Blockbuster out of business. But it didn't start this way. In 1997, Netflix launched its fixed-rate DVD-by-mail service. It was pretty cool. You could go online and put a bunch of movies in your queue, and Netflix would send you up to three movies at a time. Convenient. Nice selection. And that's exactly how Netflix went to market.

While the benefits of convenience and selection were true, they are not supercompelling. At the time, there was a Blockbuster on nearly every corner. It wasn't all that inconvenient to go out and rent a movie. And Blockbuster always had a great selection. Netflix didn't take off right away.

And then Netflix found the Point of View—the lead of its story—that mattered. What did people hate about going to Blockbuster to rent a movie? The late fees! Everybody knew the frustration of getting socked by a rental store late fee. Oh, you forgot to return the DVD on time? *Bam, late fee!* You got the DVD to the store two minutes after the deadline? *Bam, late fee!*

Netflix was so cursed by its own knowledge that it didn't even consider "no late fees" to be the lead of its story. After all, people could send their DVDs back whenever they wanted, so obviously, there were no late fees! But it wasn't so obvious to consumers. As soon as Netflix put "No Late Fees!" as the lead of its story and at the top of its marketing materials, it started taking giant bites out of Blockbuster's business—the right Point of View for the right audience.

Now, let's say Netflix were to focus its marketing efforts, not on the mass market, but specifically on cinema buffs, what would be the Point of View? "No late fees" would probably not be the most compelling factor. Instead, it should be all about "selection." That's right. They can now get that rare documentary of their favorite seventies rock band.

Get the Point of View right. And be sure to change it *every* time your audience changes.

## Action Steps: Make It Concrete

After you have developed a Point of View that is impactful and focused on change, it's time to zero in on your next challenge: converting *persuasion* into *action*. The ideal audience response should be nothing short of, "I'm in! Just tell me where to go and what to do!" So you have to *tell* people.

You must be able to point them toward a path of action. Give them a vision for the future—whether it's in the next hour or the next year—with a couple of steps they can take to make something happen. The Action Step placeholders are in the lower left corner of the Cornerstones: you'll see a General Action Step and a Specific Action Step (see Figure 6-2).

Articulating an action adds concreteness to your message, showing your audience members exactly where to go and what to do. It provides them with the clear, logical path that they need to get there. And best of all, clear action steps provide the golden nugget of accountability so that you can go back and ask, "In our last meeting, you committed to completing this task by this week. How's it going?" The Specific Action Step gets everyone working as they should in support of the Point of View. It's a huge, necessary part of our message, but we're typically pretty bad at creating it. As with the Point of View, we often don't think hard enough about the end result in a concrete way.

Case in point: Kelly worked with the CEO of an energy company who was preparing for a mid year town hall and asked him, "What do you want them to do at the end of all of this?" Kelly talked through some ideas with him, and they landed on specific ways that the business units could better align in the second half of the year. He commented, "I can't believe how much I *didn't* think about that before. I had a vision in my head, but it takes serious thought to put exactly what I want them to do into words."

Your goal is to tell your audience, both generally and specifically, what it needs to do. Don't settle on fuzzy next steps that make your message fizzle out. Understand, you don't have to provide your listeners with all the steps that lead to your ultimate goal. You may want to provide them with a set of baby steps to get them started on their journey.

First, you'll want a General Action Step: when your audience buys into your POV, what's next? A general action step is . . . general. It sounds something like, explore the subject further, compare, contrast, pilot, learn about, understand, or review the business case. Encourage your audience members to continue being open to new ideas and information. Suggest books, videos, and other resources that will guide them on this path.

Then, you'll want to give them a Specific Action Step; this should be timed, physical, and measurable. Set goals and deadlines. For example, suggest that your listeners join an organization, start an accountability group, take part in volunteerism and activism, begin a social media campaign, find a need in their neighborhood and meet it, or something similar. Give them the names and contact information of organizations with which they can connect. Give them concrete examples of other people who are taking Specific Action Steps. Give them a deadline—by Monday, by 5 p.m., by EOW, by our next meeting. Specific Action Steps can be checked off our to-do list. This is what *actually* drives action.

In February 2011, we attended our first elementary school auction. About halfway through the live auction, the auctioneer announced a special project that needed funding. He described the very specific need for $30,000 to purchase new iPads and laptops for the new computer lab. He went on to describe the specific lessons that would be conducted and how every grade level would use these devices. Every single parent in the room could see how his or her own child would benefit from this project. It wasn't just a pool of money that would be used to pay for a bunch of random school supplies. *My* kid would use an iPad to learn!

In about four minutes, the auctioneer had raised it all. Not too shabby. It took two things: (1) a specific amount of money needed and (2) a concrete image of what the money would pay for. Interestingly, the auction the following year didn't raise as much. There was no specific project, just money needed for various programs. Only about 70 percent of the amount from the previous year was raised. Coincidence? We think not.

Your message should get your audience members to raise their paddles. Move persuasion into action. Fire them up with enthusiasm, excitement, passion, and energy. Your Action Steps will show them how to leverage all that motivational energy into beneficial action for themselves and their community.

Let's get back to the voicemail sales pitch example. There wasn't a whole lot of action in that original message, other than a feeble, "Call me if you're interested." Now that we have our listeners and Point of View in place, we can consider, "When my listeners buy into the Point of View (in this example, 'Your prospects must be able to find you first'), then what do they do next?"

Check out our company website to see how we've helped others like you

**GENERAL ACTION STEP**
Figure 6-5

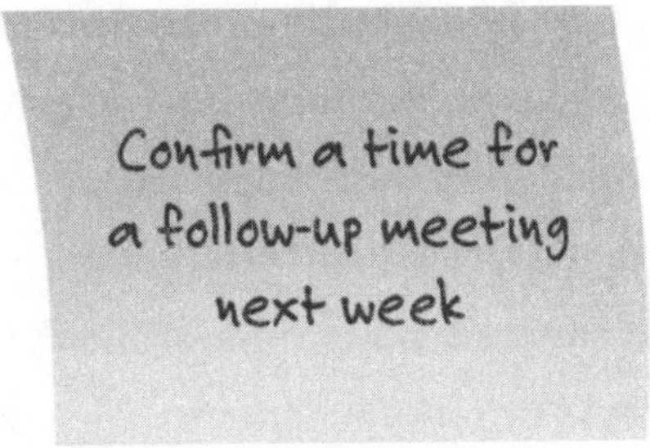

Confirm a time for a follow-up meeting next week

**SPECIFIC ACTION STEP**
Figure 6-6

Don't underestimate the power of the Action Steps (see Figures 6-5 and 6-6)! The Communicator's Roadmap is anchored by action. What differentiates the left side of the map from the right side is getting the audience *to do something* as a result of your communication experience. Including an Action Step is essential for getting across the line of information and into a realm of influence.

## Benefits: Make Them Care

The Action Steps appeal to the logical side of your listeners' brains by providing clear, step-by-step instructions. Benefits are all about getting them to care. It's your opportunity to imbue the message with more emotion (in addition to SHARPs) and shift the communication experience from Direct to Inspire. You've asked your listeners to do something (with your Action Step). Now, you'd better give them a darn good reason to do it. What's in it for them? You'll have to take a look back at your Audience Profile.

The Benefit should not be about how this action can help *you*; it should be about how this action will help *them*. Make it personal. Notice that in the fund-raising example given earlier, concreteness helped both the action (parents could "see" where their donations were going) and the benefit (they knew that it would help *their* children).

Too often, we provide a laundry list of general benefits that are far too removed to get anyone motivated to do anything. We all want to be good corporate citizens, but when we talk about ROI, increased top-line growth, greater customer satisfaction, or more streamlined work processes, it just doesn't mean a whole lot to us as individuals. You must drive that benefit down to the individual level as much as possible—think: *your* child versus the entire school system—that's where you shift from logic to emotion. And on the Communicator's Roadmap, it's how you climb up the vertical axis.

A great way to drive down to the individual level as much as possible is to go back to how you described your listeners, and present them with benefits that address their concerns, goals, and needs. For example, if you described your listeners as "risk-averse," present them with a benefit that will provide "peace of mind." If they are "budget-conscious," tell them how they can leverage an existing investment.

You might have a dozen benefits to what you're proposing, but for the purposes of framing your message, pick two.

What about that voicemail sales pitch example? In the original script, the salesperson offered "a lot" and "Internet exposure" as the benefits. Supercompelling, right? Let's go back to how we described the listener (see Figure 6-3).

Let's offer benefits that would make a small business owner's ears perk up (see Figures 6-7 and 6-8).

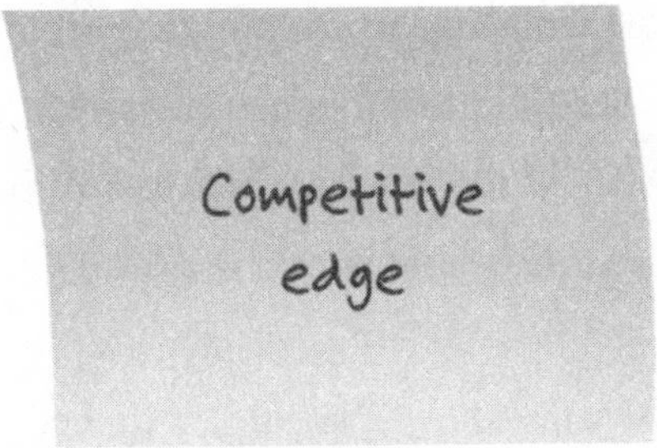

Competitive
edge

BENEFIT

Figure 6-7

**BENEFIT**
Figure 6-8

Let's take a look at how it all comes together (see Figure 6-9).

Using the Cornerstones to guide the message, the salesperson could make the message conversational by adding color around the Point of View, followed by the Action Steps and the Benefits. For example:

> Decker.com is a terrific website. The problem is that, like me, others can't find you easily, and they're probably finding your competitors before you. *Your prospects need to be able to find you first.* Our team specializes in doing just that. We help you move higher up on the search engines to direct more prospects to your website. *Check out our company website at awesomeseo.com* to give you a sense of what we've done with other coaching and consulting firms like yours. I will follow up with an e-mail proposing times for a follow-up call next week. Please let me know what works best for you, and I'll send a calendar invite. You'll find that, if you do just a few simple

## 1. Cornerstones: Focus Your Thoughts

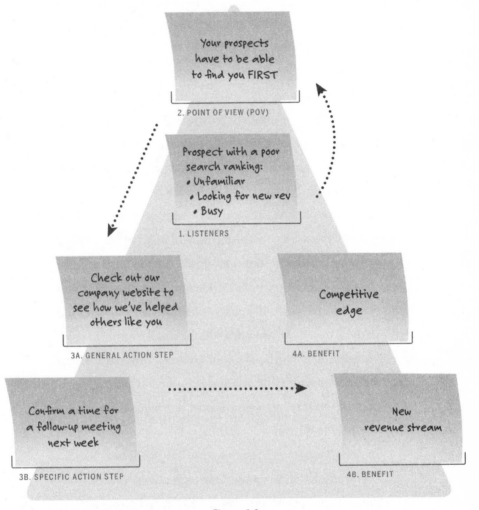

Figure 6-9

things to boost your presence, it will make it much easier for potential client to find you, *giving you a competitive edge and a new revenue stream*. I look forward to talking with you next week!

Now, that would have earned a call back—even from Kelly.

## Do Not Pass Go.

You can't pass Go and you can't collect $200 without the Cornerstones. By framing the entire message and shifting content from Self-Centered to Audience-Centered, you can move experience farther to the right on the Communicator's Roadmap, from Information to Influence.

Ingrain these Cornerstones into your messaging habits. When your boss asks you to step into a meeting and speak about the new product launch, think: Listeners, Point of View, Action, and Benefits. It's intentional practice that will shift your mindset. It will make you more action-oriented and other-centered. With a little luck, you'll be thinking of messaging this way all the time—from the conference room table to the changing table at home.

Check out this success story sent by one of our past clients, "Cole's dad." He writes:

> The messaging challenge: get Cole to change his diaper. (*Note:* It is nearly impossible to change his diaper if he doesn't want to.)
>
> **Me:** I need you to change your diaper.
>
> **Cole:** No. NO! (Adds emphasis through eye rolls and stomping.)

I remember the listener-focused framework from our training.

**Me:** Leaving your diaper on too long will give you a rash.

**Me:** Please come into your bedroom with me and lie down so that I can change your diaper.

**Me:** If you change your diaper right now, you won't get a rash and you'll be much happier.

**Me:** Come with me.

**Cole:** OK. (And with a smile)

Seriously, it really worked! Turns out that Cole is a very discerning customer of Dad's silly ideas, so I actually have to think about my POV, action, and benefit. The more compelling, the more likely it is that Cole will play along.

It all starts with the Cornerstones. Every time. Just like with Cole, the more compelling your Point of View, Action, and Benefits are, the more likely it is that your audience will play along. This first important step in the Decker Grid will begin shifting your mindset from information to influence simply by focusing on your listener. You can use the Cornerstones, alone, for a voicemail (as we saw throughout this chapter), for a quick elevator pitch, or to quickly gather your thoughts. And, if you're short on time, it's worth it to take five minutes to focus your thinking before a bigger opportunity.

When you get the Cornerstones right, planning the rest of your message becomes easy. When you have a longer talk or a bigger presentation, you need more than just the Cornerstones. They're the launch pad for an Audience-Centered message. You begin with the end in mind and just fill in the gaps. Everything you say in the main body of your message will build on your Cornerstones. Let's move on to Chapter 7, and we'll teach you how to construct the rest, complete the Decker Grid, and save time on your next big presentation, talk, event, or meeting.

---

## EXERCISES

---

**WATCH**

- Watch ad campaigns and commercials (it's worth *not* fast-forwarding through everything on your DVR). Notice how many actually have an Audience-Centered Point of View in them: Just Do It (Nike), Own Your Tomorrow (Schwab), Think Happiness (Coca-Cola).

- Notice how people approach their messages for one-on-one meetings or even a presentation. Is it about them or about you? Are they informing or updating? Or are they helping you see a big picture and moving you?

---

**THINK**

- Think about your week—all the meetings and conference calls you attended. What are you going to change as a result of the messages? What are you going to do differently? Examine how the Cornerstones may have affected those experiences.

**DO**

- Use the Cornerstones to change the way you typically prepare for an "update" kind of meeting. How can you make it more audience-focused and more action-oriented? Rather than Inform, what can you do to Influence?

- Incorporate a Point of View into your next meeting. Will your audience members agree, nod their heads, and "get" your vision of change?

- Make sure they know *exactly* what you want them to do before they leave. Specific Actions are among the more challenging elements to include.

- Hold them accountable. Be sure to check back in with your listeners after leaving them with a specific action in your next message. Did they complete it by the deadline? Did it move the ball forward?

### CHAPTER 7

# A Structure, Not a Script

*Innovation is not the product of logical thought,*
*although the result is tied to logical structure.*

—ALBERT EINSTEIN

Ben worked recently with a client we'll call Elaine, the head of the Americas for a software company. She was preparing to speak at a large industry event, and she already had two people assisting her with a script—one from PR and one from marketing. Her team members did exactly what they should have done—they prepared her with a message that was interesting and thought-provoking. The only problem was that it just wasn't Elaine's style. She became frustrated one day that the script just wasn't resonating with her. She and Ben met (without the other two) and began to have a conversation about her talk.

Ben began by walking her through the outline that the team had provided, stopping along the way to check in on key points. As soon as he asked, "How does that part sound?" Elaine would jump in, frustrated, and say, "See, those aren't my words. It just doesn't sound right."

Ben responded, "OK. How would *you* say it?"

"Well if I was just talking to you, I would say it like this. . . ."

"Great, say that!"

"Shoot! What did I just say? Get a recorder!"

Elaine realized that when the words weren't hers, she couldn't be herself, and she would become more nervous, rather than more confident. She had built enough self-awareness to recognize that speaking off the cuff and from the heart would create a far more effective experience. That, paired with (or multiplied by) the courage to take a risk and ditch the script, helped her be authentically Elaine.

Just like Elaine, you need a structure, not a script—a way to deliver a message that allows you the freedom to use your own words and to respond to the audience in the moment and off the cuff. Ultimately, when you're speaking before a large group, on a call, on a webinar, or at an important meeting, it's not about the specific words you say; it's about staying focused and organized—even when the Twitter-sphere is following.

Structure is absolutely critical to developing your message. Your audience members are seeking structure; they want to know where you're taking them. We've all sat in the audience during a presentation, wondering what the point is. Picture your audience impatiently tapping their fingers on the table until you give them direction. What do you do? With Step 1 of the Decker Grid—the Cornerstones—complete, you're on your way to building the structure that will carry your message.

## STEP 2: CREATE—
## BRAINSTORM THE SUPPORTING IDEA

There are two simple rules to keep in mind when brainstorming:

1. Don't edit. Brainstorming is about generating as many ideas as possible, without editing. We're decent at brainstorming when we're working in teams and building off of each other's ideas, but we're not so good when we're on our own. When we're too close to the material, it's harder to brainstorm because we often have a specific idea of the direction we want to go with our message. We typically edit ourselves too quickly and begin censoring ideas that have the potential to develop into a key part of our story. We quickly dismiss ideas or toss them aside, when all we should be doing is getting them on the page. At Decker, we see this most often when working one-on-one with leaders: it's often easier for an "outsider" like us to brainstorm content because we are unfamiliar with it, not because we're smarter or more creative. Before you begin, clear your mind and think big and outside the box. Your goal is quantity, not quality (at least not yet).

2. Allocate a specific amount of time. Time pressure is part of the process. Without the clock, the creative process could go on and on and on. Spend anywhere between 3 and 15 minutes, depending on the amount of time you have to prepare. The important thing is to define the time constraint and feel the crunch.

Now, with your Cornerstones in view, ask yourself, "What do my listeners need to know in order to buy into my Point of View, follow the Action Steps, and realize the Benefits?" Brainstorm the key points that support the Cornerstones. Grab your pad of sticky notes, scribble ideas as quickly as they come up, rip them off the pad, and plunk them down on the table or page in front of you. Put one idea on each sticky note. Don't worry about keeping things organized; you'll create order out of chaos later.

Consider the following:

- Key insights

- Background/current situation or problem

- Benchmarks and trends

- Examples

- Case studies/interviews

- Success stories

- Challenges

- Your solution to the problem

- Alternatives

- Changes

- Options

- Opportunities

- Recommendations

- Solutions

- What you can do

Keep brainstorming until your time is up. If the ideas are still flowing freely, take more time. It's OK. Once you have assembled a mass of ideas, you're ready for the next step.

## STEP 3: CLUSTER—
## ORGANIZE YOUR THOUGHTS

We're not quite ready to edit all these ideas, yet. Now it's time to organize them to make sense of it all. The clustering step will allow you to edit them much more effectively in our final step. Cluster your similar ideas together. For example, several ideas may be related to the financial impact of what you're proposing. Put those in one cluster. Maybe there are a few sticky notes that provide details on the proposed solution. Put those into one cluster, and so on.

After you're done clustering, you may realize that you have a few sticky notes that don't quite fit into your existing clusters. No problem. Don't force it. Ideas that don't fit into a cluster might be used later. Or if, after thinking about your listeners, you realize that an idea doesn't apply (maybe it's too high or too low a level of detail, or a tangent that's not worth following), then you can put that sticky note aside.

Once you've clustered your ideas together, it's time to find the main idea of each cluster. You probably already have a sticky note with the main idea, with all of the remaining sticky notes in that cluster supporting that idea. Underline the main idea within each cluster. If not, go ahead and add a sticky note with an appropriate label for the cluster. These underlined labels will be your Key Points. The ideas clustered under these labels will be your Subpoints. Think of each Key Point as a claim that you are making to build your Cornerstones and the Subpoints as the evidence to support it.

Review each cluster. These clusters will often trigger more ideas, so take three minutes for additional brainstorming. Assign your new sticky notes to the appropriate clusters.

Now you're ready to start the final editing or composing of your message.

## STEP 4: COMPOSE—
## EDIT YOUR FINAL MESSAGE

The Decker Grid follows the old adage, "Tell 'em what you're gonna tell 'em. Tell 'em. And then tell 'em what you told 'em." In the Compose step, your job is to pare it down to your very best ideas and organize your message for maximum persuasion and impact (see Figure 7-1). Start by composing the central part of your message, the Main Body. You can compose the opening and closing later.

### 4. Compose: The Decker Grid

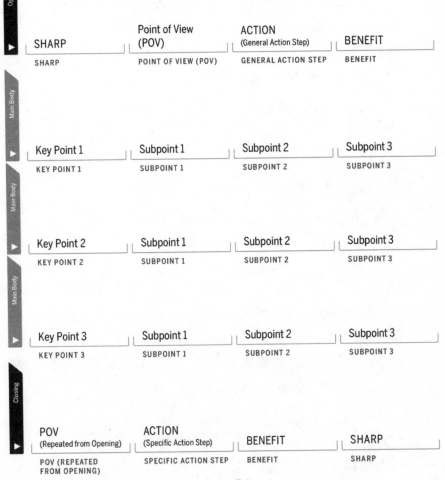

Figure 7-1

Focus on the Rule of Three: things are best remembered and organized in threes. The Latin phrase *omni trium perfectum*—everything that comes in threes is perfect—echoes this. The Rule of Three leverages brevity and pattern recognition. Humans are really good at pattern recognition, and three is the smallest number needed to create a pattern. Add a fourth item to any trio and retention plummets. As Muriel Humphrey once said to her husband, Vice President Hubert H. Humphrey, "Remember, Hubert, a speech doesn't have to be eternal to be immortal."

You'll notice the Rule of Three everywhere:

- Stop, drop, and roll

- Green light, yellow light, red light

- Life, liberty, and the pursuit of happiness

- The Three Little Pigs, Three Blind Mice, Three Amigos

- Veni, vidi, vici

In storytelling, the Rule of Three can be seen in the classic three-act structure, where Act I is the setup, Act II is the confrontation, and Act III is the Resolution. Let's take a favorite movie of ours, *Gladiator*, as an example.

Act I. After waging a successful war on behalf of his emperor, the general Maximus makes his way home to his family. But the emperor's son, Commodus, sees

Maximus as a threat, leads a coup against his father, and kills Maximus's family.

Act II. Maximus survives slavery and makes a name for himself as a gladiator in northern Africa before he arrives in Rome, where he becomes a great gladiator and wins the crowd. He rallies supporters and develops a plan to overthrow Commodus for the future of Rome.

Act III. Maximus kills Commodus and restores Rome to order with the establishment of a republic.

Setup, confrontation, resolution. There you go. Two and a half hours in five sentences. The point is that we're all familiar with this three-act structure, and it provides a great framework for creating persuasive content for a sales pitch, motivating change in an organization, or launching a new product. Similar structures often used in business presentations are situation, complication, resolution and background, solution, next steps. The key is to limit yourself to three key points to avoid data dumps of information. You need to be ruthless in prioritizing the very best support for your message. Then, put it into a logical flow. Structure your talk so that you build to your strongest and most important Key Point.

In the main body of the Decker Grid (the middle three lines in Figure 7-1), you'll see a layout for your presentation. That layout provides spaces for you to position your best three Key Points (the underlined, cluster headings)—and *only* three Key Points. To the side of each of those Key Points is a row of three spaces. Choose your three best supporting Subpoints for each of those three Key Points (your Subpoints come from within the cluster).

As you Compose, you'll find that the Decker Grid gives you enormous freedom and flexibility. You can trade Subpoints, move ideas around, and rearrange your Key Points in seconds just by moving your sticky notes.

## Hook 'Em: What's the Beginning of Your Message?

Once you have the main body of your message, it's time to go back to the beginning and prepare the opening of your talk. A good opening is critical to setting the tone for your message and giving your listeners a reason to listen. Too often, messages begin without purpose or direction, where the speaker starts with something like, "I'm so glad to be here. Today I will be talking about X," and continues for two more minutes of opening comments, leaving the audience impatient and giving people an excuse to tune out. We call this type of introduction an LBOW: lovely bunch of words. Many of our clients assume that they have to ease their way into the ask. They dump information, try to prove themselves and their proposals, and then expect the audience to sign on the dotted line.

Instead, craft an opening that provides a direction to your message and it will prepare your listeners' minds for action.

They'll think, "OK, I see where this is going, and I am going to be asked to do something about it." Throughout the message your listeners will be looking for proof and supporting material, and if you've provided those things, your listeners will be far more likely to do as you ask and take the specific action step at the end.

You simply need to move the sticky notes from your Cornerstones to the opening line of the Decker Grid. You'll take your Point of View, General Action Step, and Benefit, and put them in the labeled placeholders in the opening line. (Skip the SHARP for now—we'll come back to that shortly.)

## End with a Bang: Close Strong

End with a bang, not a whimper. The closing structure outlined in the Decker Grid is easy to create, and it's extremely effective when it's delivered. Sum up the most important parts of your message: restate your Point of View (yes, the exact same one you used in your opening line), and then share your Specific Action Step and Benefit from the Cornerstones.

Take a look at your completed Decker Grid. Your message is relevant to your listeners; it's focused, structured, well organized, and action-oriented. Now for an important question: Is it memorable?

This is a moment of truth that we don't often consider when developing our messages. Your audience is inundated every hour of the day with new information, some of which competes directly for the time and attention required for your ideas, initiatives, and proposals. How will your message be remembered over all the others? How will you stand out in a crowded marketplace of ideas in your organization or industry? Here's where the SHARPs come in.

We're living in an attention economy. The average attention span for an adult is a measly eight seconds (we're only two seconds better than our kids). This doesn't mean that you can only hold someone's attention for eight seconds; it means that you can lose it in eight seconds.[1] SHARPs become your currency.

Your listener's attention is highest at the beginning of your message and at the end of your message, and looks like Figure 7-2 if we graph it over time.

**ATTENTION SPAN OVER TIME**

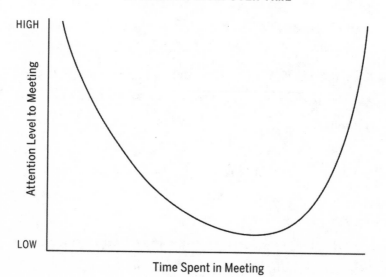

Figure 7-2

You can leverage your listener's high attention by ensuring that the opening and closing are as memorable as possible; these are perfect places to insert SHARPs. Begin with a story, an analogy, a quote, or a big statistic. A great opening SHARP will also set you at ease within the first 30 to 90 seconds, the most stressful part of any talk or presentation.

While you will naturally have your listeners' attention in the beginning and at the end, this does not mean that you can just allow their attention to dip in the middle. So take a look at your Decker Grid and find out where you can add a SHARP to highlight a key point, or show a visual image to make your evidence more concrete. It's up to you to alter the attention graph by using SHARPs throughout your message, making it look more like Figure 7-3.

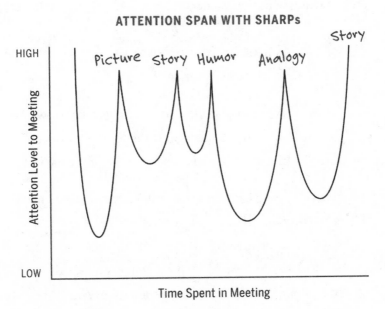

Figure 7-3

# THE DECKER GRID IN ACTION

Let's go through the full Decker Grid system with an example. Kelly worked on a message with the general counsel and the senior vice president of compliance for a large energy company, who had the dubious honor of conducting a mandatory 45-minute compliance training session for the leadership team of approximately 35 people. Compliance training is right up there with waiting in line at the DMV. Typically, this is an experience that's headed straight for the bowels of the Inform quadrant on our Communicator's Roadmap. But we can do more!

Rather than rattling through the latest compliance checklist, they worked on shifting to an Audience-Centered message, starting with the listeners.

## Step 1: Cornerstones—
## Focus Your Message

*Listeners.* A group of leaders who are big thinkers, who genuinely want to do the right thing for the business, but who are incredibly busy and stretched for time.

*Point of View.* "Compliance is important, and you need to be covered." That's the bottom line, and it's certainly what the company wanted them to do. "Just check the box and we can make this whole thing end quickly." That would have, at best, elicited a response of, "I'll do it because I have to." How could we make this a better

## 1. Cornerstones: Focus Your Thoughts

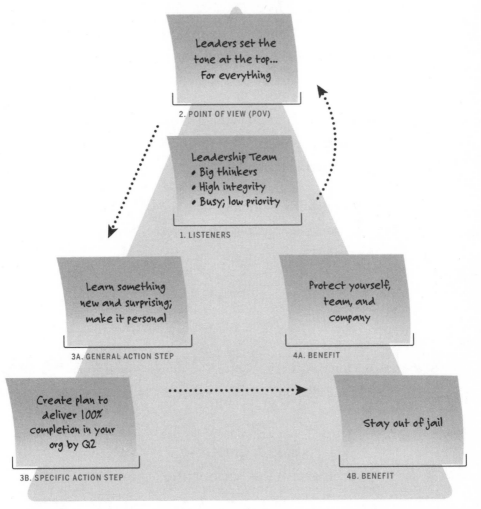

Figure 7-4

experience for the listeners? How could we get them to believe in its importance and motivated to do it? Shift the lead of the story away from the training itself. Focus instead on the leaders in the room. Suppose the Point of View was, "As leaders, we set the tone at the top. For everything, including compliance." That's certainly a higher call than "Compliance is important," and it was more likely to motivate the leaders and shift them from a response of "I have to" to "I want to."

*General Action.* Learn something new and surprising. Try to make it personal. What's a situation in which this would apply to your team?

*Specific Action.* Think through how you will position this with your team to deliver 100 percent completion by the end of Q2.

*Benefits.* Protect yourself, your team, and our company. Stay out of jail.

Cornerstones. Check. Figure 7-4 shows how it looks, sticky notes and all.

## Step 2: Create— Brainstorm the Supporting Idea

Now, what about the rest of the message? Kelly and the two executives set the timer for five minutes and had a flurry of ideas, anything and everything that would support the Cornerstones. They asked, "What does the leadership team need to know to buy into the Point of View, take the Action, and realize the Benefit?" Figure 7-5 shows what they came up with.

## 2. Create: Brainstorm Supporting Ideas

Figure 7-5

## Step 3: Cluster—
## Organize Your Thoughts

Quickly organize the ideas into clusters (see Figure 7-6). Identify one idea as the Key Point and underline it. Use the others as the supporting ideas for the Key Point.

### 3. Cluster: Organize Your Thoughts

Figure 7-6

## Step 4: Compose—
## Edit Your Final Message

The final step was to organize all the ideas into a logical structure. They chose to begin with the broad message concerning the importance of compliance and then move on to what was specific to the company and finally to the individual teams. Once the main body was crafted, they completed the opening and closing by bringing sticky notes from the Cornerstones onto the Decker Grid (see Figure 7-7).

## 4. Compose: Edit Your Final Message

Figure 7-7

Finally, they brainstormed a few SHARPs that could be used. Kelly encouraged them to reflect on their own experi-

## 4. Compose: Add SHARPs

Figure 7-8

ences. The general counsel immediately cited an analogy that always stuck with her.

Figure 7-8 shows their final Decker Grid.

## DELIVER WITH THE DECKER GRID

The Decker Grid is designed to help you stay focused and organized throughout your message. Remember that it's not important for you to choose the precise words for every transition. You will be able to pick up a thought from your trigger words, then speak to it in a conversational manner. You will come across as natural, authentic, and connected, as opposed to scripted, stiff, and robotic.

When it comes to delivering your message, use the Decker Grid as notes that you can refer to. Leave it on a lectern or table in front of you. You won't get lost because you will not be reading; you'll be communicating. If you happen to hit a snag and forget what comes next, a quick glance at your trigger words will get you instantly back on track, and your audience will never notice that anything was wrong.

Here's the result of the compliance example we've been discussing. The general counsel began,

*"I had a mentor who used to tell me that everything he did as a leader was amplified. It's as if he had a megaphone attached permanently to his mouth and the spotlight was always on him. As senior leaders, we set the tone at the top. Each of our associates takes cues from us on how to dress, how to conduct*

*themselves in a meeting, what's the appropriate way to challenge an idea. And we rise to the occasion. We walk the talk. We participate in the "Get Moving" initiative and wear pedometers every day. We show our commitment to our communities by participating in volunteer events, and we show our leadership in our daily meetings. There's one place where we don't . . . compliance."* And then she showed the stats on how many people in the room had actually completed the mandatory training! She had their attention, and heads were nodding—the exact result you're looking for after delivering a strong introduction.

Then, the SVP of compliance took over and bridged to the Point of View, Action, and Benefits. *"You set the tone. It is our duty as the leadership team to set the right tone at the top for compliance. Learn something surprising, think about how to apply this specifically to your teams, and have some fun. Stay out of jail. Orange is not the new black!"*

They went on to set up what they would cover for the day: "Today we'll address three things: (1) when bad things happen to good people; (2) surprising truths and new policies that you need to know; and (3) how you can talk to your team to ensure compliance."

They balanced the serious nature of risk with some humor throughout, engaged the audience, and received a standing ovation at the end—all because they intentionally mapped and changed the experience.

# THE DECKER GRID FOR ANY SITUATION

Whether you're leading an organization, mobilizing a project team, or planning a client meeting, you'll find that the Decker Grid is flexible and versatile enough to use in any situation. An audience-centered message makes a difference every time. We'll leave you with two examples of common situations so that you can further apply the grid to any of your upcoming messages.

## Example: Sales Pitch

When we tell any salesperson, veteran or newbie, that he can close more deals with one simple tool, he is immediately interested. The good news is, whether you are selling a product, a service, or an experience, the same tool will reframe your message so it's about the person who is listening—and it will elicit faster action. This tool is the Decker Grid.

Here's a technology sales scenario: the people in your audience think that new technology is nice to have, but they don't feel any urgency. This example applies to almost any company—a financial services company, a power company, a telecom company with a lot of legacy services, a start-up that is using a little bit of this or a little bit of that—that could make the listeners' processes and legacy systems more streamlined and more efficient. Take a look at how all the pieces come together: the Point of View, Action Steps, Benefits, Key Points, and Subpoints (see Figure 7-9).

## Decker Grid: Technology Sales Pitch

| Opening | | | |
|---|---|---|---|
| Integration Analogy | Tech Integration is critical: systems must have one brain | Think of one-stop access to client info | Access to the info you need to serve |
| SHARP | POINT OF VIEW (POV) | GENERAL ACTION STEP | BENEFIT |

| Main Body | | | |
|---|---|---|---|
| Why tech matters more than ever | Megatrends: Cloud. Mobile. Social. | What could this mean to your client? | How it works |
| KEY POINT 1 | SUBPOINT 1 | SUBPOINT 2 | SUBPOINT 3 |

| Main Body | | | |
|---|---|---|---|
| Proven success | Compare vs. benchmark at 14% | Examples: Customer 1 & Customer 2 | Questions? |
| KEY POINT 2 | SUBPOINT 1 | SUBPOINT 2 | SUBPOINT 3 |

| Main Body | | | |
|---|---|---|---|
| Begin the partnership | Client Testimonial | Next steps | Contract Review |
| KEY POINT 3 | SUBPOINT 1 | SUBPOINT 2 | SUBPOINT 3 |

| Closing | | | |
|---|---|---|---|
| True Integration is critical | Feedback: List of requests by Q3 | Win-win for team and clients | Story: Integrating Your Team |
| POV (REPEATED FROM OPENING) | SPECIFIC ACTION STEP | BENEFIT | SHARP |

Figure 7-9

The best sales pitches get as granular as possible when it comes to how the product or service you are selling will benefit your specific audience. The more targeted your message is, the better the chance that your listeners will nod their heads in agreement. And you can see that by keeping your presentation focused on your audience, there's even space for the client to ask questions. The Decker Grid is so flexible that it can be used to prepare you to fly solo, as well as foster a dialogue with your audience.

### Example: Performance Review

If you're delivering a performance review, the goal is for it to be *other-centered*—centered on the employee who is being reviewed. Consider that person overall and vis-à-vis his thoughts and expectations going into the review. A performance review is a great opportunity to use the Decker Grid and build your discussion points.

This message must be specifically crafted for the individual employee—focused on his needs, wants, goals, and attributes. Keep in mind that although you will be the one driving the agenda and setting the tone, a great performance review is a conversation, not a monologue. See how we have built conversation pieces into the grid template in Figure 7-10.

## DITCH THE SCRIPT

The audience latches on to structure. Get focused, stay organized, and ditch your script. Our Point of View for you: shift the way you think about all your communication situations. Here's our Action Step: test it for yourself this week. Use the Decker Grid to prepare for a meeting or conference call. Ask

## Decker Grid: Performance Review

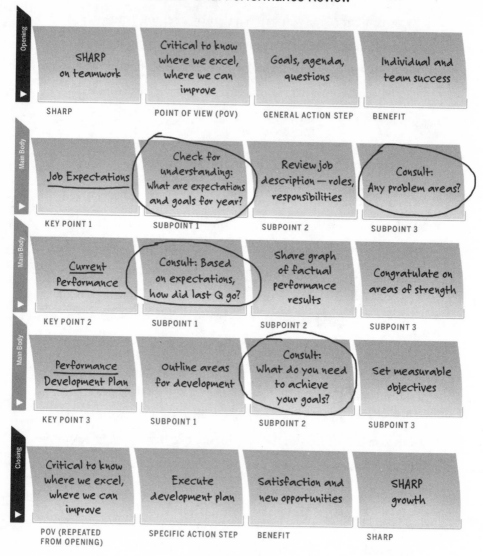

Figure 7-10

yourself: Have I constructed a message that meets the needs of my listeners? Have I stated my Point of View clearly, so that my listeners can buy into it? Have I stated the Action in such a way that my listeners know exactly what to do in response to my message? And are the Benefits clear so that my listeners will be enthusiastic and motivated?

And the Benefits? You'll become more persuasive, effective, influential, and, yes, even inspiring in every communication situation, every day.

## EXERCISES

**WATCH**

- Notice the Rule of Three in action, from corporate speeches to the three-act structure in a movie.

- Watch and listen for speakers who sound conversational in their delivery. Chances are that they are unscripted.

- Look for the moments when your attention drops in a meeting. How does the speaker recapture it?

**THINK**

- Think about your last three meetings. What was the speaker's Point of View? What was the *one* thing she wanted you to walk away with?

- What stands out from the last formal presentation that you watched? Was it a

SHARP? How did it help you remember the Point of View or Key Point of the message?

------------------------------------------------------------

**DO**

- Plan your next message using the Decker Grid. It could be for a conference call, an internal meeting, or a client presentation.

- Grab people's attention! Get rid of the LBOWs in your next talk, and begin with a SHARP!

------------------------------------------------------------

### CHAPTER 8

# Navigate Your Experience

*If you don't know where you're going,*
*you'll end up someplace else.*

—YOGI BERRA

Now that you have a firm understanding of how to move across the vertical axis of connection and the horizontal axis of content, it's time to zero in: How do you create an experience and bring it all together?

We recognize that our default leaves us somewhere in the Inform quadrant, where we have more information to dump, news to report, updates to share, or items to cross off our list. When push comes to shove, how do you harness all the tools (the Behaviors of Trust, SHARPs, the Cornerstones, and the Decker Grid) to create your ideal communications experience?

The following are a few examples of situations in which you may find yourself.

📍 Destination: **Entertain**

Figure 8-1

## THE PANEL DISCUSSION: INFORM TO ENTERTAIN

At a Clinton Global Initiative session in September 2013, there was a morning panel called Mobilizing for Impact. The panelists included Bono, the lead singer of U2 and cofounder of ONE and (RED); Mo Ibrahim, the founder and chairman of Mo Ibrahim Foundation; Khalida Brohi, the founder and executive director of Sughar Empowerment Society, Giving Women Wings in Pakistan; Christine Lagarde, the managing director of the International Monetary Fund; and Sheryl Sandberg, the chief operating officer of Facebook. The panelists were seated. The audience was waiting. The moderator of the panel was Bill Clinton himself, but he was running late.

It got to a point where the panelists were wearing polite smiles and beginning to fidget awkwardly in silence. Rather than look at his watch, Bono took the opportunity to add humor and energy to the panel (see Figure 8-1). Handing his microphone to Sheryl Sandberg, he trotted over to the empty moderator's chair and did an impression of Bill Clinton that lasted a little over a minute. He nailed Clinton's accent, speech patterns, and cadence. Relieved, the panelists and the audience members burst into laughter. It was a pretty good impersonation! Clearly, it wasn't Bono's first time ad-libbing on the mike. By the time Clinton walked onto the stage, the audience was already warm and laughing.

What did Bono consider? The experience. He increased emotional connection by adding humor, engaging with the people in the room. Most of us wouldn't do what Bono did. It's both high risk and high reward. But it was worth it. Here's what we can learn: on your next panel, move from Inform to Entertain (see Figure 8-2).

Starting Position: **Inform**

Destination: **Entertain**

Figure 8-2

The setting is an industry conference or event in which you have been invited to sit on a panel as a subject-matter expert. The audience wants to hear your unique perspective. The situation is intended to be about you, so rather than just sit there and Inform, how can you boost the experience?

The two of us recently worked as a tag team to help prepare two clients for a consumer panel on wearable technology. The technology was still in its infancy, and the co-product managers were excited about describing all the features and functions. They wanted to talk all about the science behind what they had created, and how all the pieces worked together. When we did a practice panel with them, it seemed as if they had completely forgotten that the whole appeal of their product was in the way consumers would experience it.

We knew they needed to amplify their emotional connection in a big way in order to hit a home run on their panel. You can do the same.

## How You Get There

To move up to Entertain and increase your emotional connection, you have two tools:

1. The Behaviors of Trust

- *Make the connection with your eyes.* Too often, panelists just look at the moderator when they respond, and neglect their audience. It's tough at first because your natural tendency is to look at the person who asked you the question. Instead, look out into the audience. Think of the 80/20 rule: give 80 percent of your focus to the audience and 20 percent to the moderator. Involve and connect with those who are sitting in the room. Practice eye communication with the audience, holding your gaze for a full five seconds with people from all parts of the room.

- *Have fun!* Banter with the other panelists, and play off of them. Show lightness. Smile. And not just during your intro. It's amazing how quickly our faces can become furrowed and serious when we're talking about our expertise. Audiences are drawn to those who have passion and lightness. So let your natural self out. And (yes, it bears repeating) smile!

- *Keep them tuned in with energy.* Lean forward in your chair, bringing your energy toward the audience. Our energy levels tend to dip when we are seated, so be sure you are projecting your voice and using gestures to let your energy shine through. Too often, panelists are stoic and flat. Audience members are more apt to pay attention when we look as if we care about what we're saying!

- *Be aware of your behavioral habits when you are listening, too.* After all, you aren't always speaking during a panel. Do you pick at your fingers or tend to frown? Do you lose your posture? Don't look bored; your nonverbal behaviors will speak volumes. You are still part of the communications experience. (Remember Joe Biden during the 2012 vice presidential debate, grimacing, rolling his eyes, and shaking his head while his challenger was responding? We do, and we always bring it up as an example of what *not* to do.) You're always on!

2. SHARPs. It's easy to lead with logic. In these panels, you want to prove yourself and prove your point, and it's easy to stick to the logical angle. Instead of

just giving a straight or abstract answer, do you have an example that could explain it better? Have some SHARPs in your back pocket ready to go. The best kinds are concrete examples that help the audience "see" what you're discussing. Not only will this help you be clearer, but your audience will probably remember your point long after the panel is over.

Consider telling a story. Give yourself bonus points if it shows vulnerability (a time when something didn't go as planned), as it will increase your connection. Or use humor, but keep in mind that this is not the time to seize the open mike and try out a new stand-up gig. Make sure you add value if you decide to go outside the lines to liven it up.

For the panel on wearable technologies, we got our panelists to tell stories and not just any stories, different little "aha" moments that would resonate with the audience of nonscientists and nonengineers. They also told a story about using the technology while riding their bikes. When they talked about all the scenic details, the story came alive. Almost anyone can relate to the experience of riding a bike.

Refer to your fellow panelists. It is a challenge to listen to four other panelists, but it's great when you can do it well. If you can show rapport with the other panelists, it provides critical links for your audience. You'll be able to play off their remarks and add unique value and insights of your own. If you're thinking solely of what you're going to say next, you may miss an opportunity.

Destination: **Inspire**

Figure 8-3

# THE KICKOFF:
## MOVE YOUR CALL TO *INSPIRE*

It's January again. Same three days. Same people. Same place (Vegas). Same order in the line up: CEO, CFO, VP of sales, CMO, and chief product officer. It's the same drill, even if it *is* a new year with a new theme. From "Rev It Up in '99 (with a NASCAR Connection)," to "Out of This World in 2001," "2007: The Next Generation," "Revolution in 2010," and "Take it to 11 in 2011," the annual theme is meant to motivate anywhere from 500 to 3,000 people.

Here's the way it typically rolls out: main stage presentations, followed by breakout sessions. It's mandatory attendance, and while it's tempting to do a slew of updates, there's nothing memorable about that. Change the experience by stepping up to the plate and aiming for Inspire (see Figure 8-3).

Starting Position: **Inform**

Destination: **Inspire**

Figure 8-4

Mike (not his real name) was the lead product manager for a software development company. As he was getting ready for his sales kickoff, he came to us and said, "Look, I have the presentation thing down after years of consulting at McKinsey. I can drive action. What I need help with, though, is how do I inspire my audience?"

Mike had a great voice, the kind you really want to listen to, and he was a very likable guy. There were a few things breaking his connection with his audience, though. He stood with his arms crossed over his chest, and he spoke really fast. He also had this habit of looking down in between thoughts. It wasn't the kind of thing you'd notice right away, but he did it consistently, which became distracting. Mike was a bit in his own world.

On the content side, Mike was superorganized, just as you would expect any consultant to be. However, in order to shift his talk from "you have to" sell my new software to "you want to" sell my new software, Mike needed to focus less on the features and benefits of his new data-synthesizing software. To really fire up his sales team and get them on board, he needed to share more details about how his software could affect something bigger (see Figure 8-4).

How could he take it one step further? Mike needed to shift his Point of View to something that would get his sales team nodding and get them excited about selling his new product. Mike needed to shift to a higher call to action. How was his software capable of making a difference in the world?

Well, for starters, it was helping to provide clean drinking water in the developing world. It was also saving lives because surgeons had greater access to essential information while their patients were on the operating table. As if that weren't enough, it was enabling data to be used more efficiently to get kids to school. Yes, the same data-synthesizing software could affect healthcare, education, and transportation. These amazing solutions made the team proud to be affiliated with Mike's new software. They could really feel that they were a part of it when he told stories of the surgeons, patients, inner-city children, and mothers who would benefit from using the software. When Mike shared these SHARPs, the details humanized the way the software could be integrated into people's lives. He was able to get the sales force to understand that it wasn't just about selling a software license; it was about being a part of something bigger.

## How You Get There

Use your tools to go up the vertical axis and increase connection.

If you are one of 10 or 15 speakers who are taking the stage, you'll really want to stand out. Challenge yourself to use all the behavioral tools around energy (posture, movement, gestures, facial expression, voice and vocal variety) to be more engaging and more memorable than your colleagues.

Make the connection with your eyes. When the audience grows to more than 200 people, we tend to fall back into our old habits. Sometimes we scan the crowd, or just focus on one section. Remember how important it is to include everyone in the audience. Hold your gaze for a full five seconds, and look at people from all parts of the room.

For the message, shift from self-centered content to audience-centered content. Use the Cornerstones—Point of View, Action Steps and Benefits—and make them all specific to your listener.

Pick a Point of View and stick to it. During a kickoff, they hear so many different things from so many different people. What's the one key thing you want them to take away? It reminds us of a trial lawyer who said, "If I say ten things, I've said nothing. If I say one thing, they'll remember it." Think about your next kickoff that way. What is the one thing you want them to remember?

To really make sure it's inspiring, add a SHARP that links to your Cornerstones. This way, you get the double benefit of emotional connection and Audience-Centered action. Remember John McGee teaching his daughter to drive a stick shift (from Chapter 5)? His team did, for years. This is the goal of your kickoff.

## Inspire at a Kickoff to the Policy Makers

Eva, an executive at a Fortune 100 company, was traveling across the country to launch a new initiative that would affect government, politicians, and decision makers. As often happens at large companies, Eva's communications team worked on a standard message for this wide-reaching launch that was straightforward and easy to understand. One problem was that the team was using bland examples. The same examples that generally worked in "any major city" weren't going to resonate particularly well with the Chicago audience. The home of deep-dish pizza, the El, the Magnificent Mile, a green river on St. Patrick's Day, WGN, 'da Bears, the Cubs, and the coldest darn winters—there are many things that are unique to Chicago. She would need to appeal more emotionally if she was to have any hope of making it to Inspire.

Ben worked with Eva to focus on how to cast a vision specifically for the city of Chicago. He asked, What would this launch mean to Chicagoans? How would it affect Chicago? What changes would people notice? How would they be able to measure? As the answers started flowing, so did the sticky notes. Suddenly, Eva had shifted her message to become Chicago-centric. The result? People were inspired! By creating that emotional connection through all the specific things that her audience knew inside and out, Eva made them consider what Chicago *could be*. When she shared what it could be, she got them on board.

## TOWN HALL: DON'T JUST UPDATE—MOTIVATE

The town hall typically happens with a webcast across the company in multiple locations. Top executives speak; employees at all levels have a chance to submit questions. Generally, much to our dismay, the goal of these meetings is to update everyone at the same time. Where does the company stand with respect to revenue, targets, customer service ratings, and NPS scores? Basically, it's an onslaught of updates and metrics. Every time we hear the word *update*, it makes us cringe. What would be more ideal? Increasing engagement, ownership, and inspiration, of course. Everyone's listening, so don't miss the opportunity to inspire. Give people something actionable, something motivating.

Starting Position: **Direct**

Destination: **Inspire**

Figure 8-5

## The Town Hall at Crunch Time

Dennis Woodside, then the CEO of Motorola Mobility, is a great example of a leader who shifted his town hall experience from Direct to Inspire (see Figure 8-5). Across the company, his reputation was very intense. Dennis was a driver. He had a strong work ethic, was supersmart, and had high expectations. His team anticipated that he would bark at them during the town hall—and rightfully so.

It was time to get the company's new product out, and it was behind schedule. Everyone was tired. There had been lots of late nights and a slew of snags along the way, with the deadline rapidly approaching. Dennis needed to direct, as there was still so far to go. It would have been so easy for him to deliver a "need to do this," "have to do that," kind of talk.

Instead, Dennis realized that he had to get more inspirational. It was 2013, and the Chicago Blackhawks had just won the Stanley Cup. After being down two games to one, the Blackhawks had won three games in a row to defeat the Boston Bruins and win the NHL's most coveted trophy. When Dennis addressed his team members, he used the Blackhawks as an example, recognizing that his team, too, was down—and needed to be up. He asked his team members to consider the next 60 to 90 days of crunch time before the product rollout as their Stanley Cup.

In doing so, Dennis showed lightness (he was a hockey fan following the Cup series, after all!), and he smiled way more than normal. He was able to dial up his emotional connection, inspiring hope with his analogy. Together, they could see the light at the end of the tunnel, and they heard the refrain "We are the champions" echoing in their heads.

## WHEN THE EXPLETIVE HITS THE FAN: NAVIGATE TO DIRECT

When things are trending the wrong way, sometimes it's necessary to deliver a wake-up call. If you have high likability and a high emotional connection with people, sometimes you have to get down to it and just give directions. It's more rare than common, and we'd argue that you should always start by inspiring rather than barking orders. But sometimes, you need to navigate to Direct (see Figure 8-6).

### Destination: **Direct**

Figure 8-6

The best time to navigate to Direct is in crisis management. Think of a large building in a disaster or a power or telecom outage when your e-commerce website goes down. You don't need to foster an emotional connection; you just need action, and you need it quickly. In that instance, be directive. Get everyone together—or on the phone—ASAP, and be crisp and action-oriented. Tell people what to do.

Starting Position: **Inform**

Destination: **Direct**

Figure 8-7

## Making Action from Data

We recently worked with a hotshot PhD—let's call him Shankar—who is in charge of the quality and safety side of a large hospital system. Shankar loves data, which is a good thing, because a large part of his day-to-day role is analyzing data. He is the go-to guy who regularly reports to the board committee that is responsible for overseeing safety and quality for his hospital chain. In these committee meetings, Shankar's role is to inform the committee of the chain's numbers in relation to industry standards. All he wants the committee members to do is to check off their due diligence boxes and be able to say, "We've done our fiduciary responsibility." He just wants to inform them.

To get Shankar to drive more action and shift his content from Inform to Direct, we focused his message on the purpose of what they were all doing (see Figure 8-7). We zoomed out for that 30,000-foot view. All of their collective work—and all of the numbers that Shankar was sharing—reflected actual patients. Shankar used a new Point of View: "We need to continue to accelerate the improvement of our quality and safety." That Point of View, alone, showed momentum. But rather than dissecting data points, it pushed an idea, an idea with traction. This shift made Shankar's data-rich content *other-centered*. It was all about the patients. From here, he could share the data that he had collected and analyzed while also making it actionable. It enabled the board committee to engage with his numbers. He asked them to look for good things, giving the committee a way to be involved, instead of asking them to sit on the sidelines and watch the stats tick by them. Instead of a CYA, defensive, informing talk, it became a directive—telling the committee members what he wanted them to do.

Shankar had a really tough time getting from Inform to Direct. And he's not alone. Many analytical folks—scientists, scholars, financial modelers, doctors, even pastors, believe it or not—have a tough time shifting their talks so that they affect the members of their audience.

## How You Get There

Rather than rely on the numbers to speak for themselves, find an angle for how and why your data and your analysis relate to your audience. Whether you've got a committee meeting, a research report, a results reveal, anything regulatory, or an academic forum, the accountability and action that go along with a benefit will make a world of difference.

Challenge yourself to find at least two to three hot spots, points of reference, or action steps that people can do something with. What are the ways in which people can use your data? How can your findings change lives, specifically, the lives of your audience? Focus on these and use your data to support them rather than making data the whole story.

## MAP IT!

Throughout this chapter, we showed how real leaders—like you—made small tweaks and deliberately reframed their messages to get to different places on the Communicator's Roadmap.

Whatever your communication experience, think about your desired outcome. Then back up to make sure that you arrive at your destination. The keys to the Communicator's Roadmap are intention and flexibility. You can achieve greater emotional connection by using the Behaviors of Trust and SHARPs. It's important to practice. Shift your lens.

Spend the extra time to focus on your listeners and customize your message. What's the experience you want to create for them?

--------------------------------------------------------
## EXERCISES
--------------------------------------------------------

**WATCH**

- Watch the person who is leading your next meeting. At the end of the meeting, pinpoint what experience that person created.

- Learn from leaders who do something unexpected and deliberately shift the experience the way Bono used unexpected humor on the panel to move from Inform to Entertain.

--------------------------------------------------------

**THINK**

- Revisit your pivot points, the skills from Chapter 4 that will make the biggest difference in how you come across. Think of specific behaviors that you will change.

--------------------------------------------------------

**DO**

- Record yourself on video. Map the experience that you created. If you could do it again, what would you change? On which axis do you need to put more of your effort: emotional connection or content?

- Look at your calendar for the next week. Map each engagement: for example, your conference call on Tuesday, your staff meeting on Thursday, and your client call on Friday.

- Share more of yourself in the work environment. Push yourself to be vulnerable and boost your emotional connection.

### CHAPTER 9

# The 10X Communicator

*If you're not doing some things that are crazy,*
*then you're doing the wrong things.*

—LARRY PAGE

There will always be a new destination to map, a new experience to create, a new audience to move, and an end result that transforms the audience response from, "OK, I'll do it because I have to," to, "I'm in! Because I *want* to."

It takes work. Your effort is well worth it. In this concluding chapter, we'll weave it all together.

First, you must recognize the opportunity.

Next, you must put in the work. You'll need serious commitment and a healthy dose of courage.

Finally, you must answer the call. It's a big one. Get ready.

## RECOGNIZE THE OPPORTUNITY

On May 25, 1961, JFK stood before Congress and proclaimed, "This nation should commit itself to achieving the goal, before the decade is out, of landing a man on the moon and returning him safely to the earth."

In *Built to Last*, Jim Collins and Jerry Porras use JFK's vision as an example of what they call a Big Hairy Audacious Goal (BHAG)—a goal so bold, extreme, and audacious that the odds of success seem questionable, yet the very riskiness of the quest energizes and motivates those who commit to the goal. Collins and Porras wrote, "The most optimistic scientific assessment of the moon mission's chances for success in 1961 was fifty-fifty and most experts were, in fact, more pessimistic. . . . Given the odds, such a bold commitment was, at the time, outrageous."[1]

Could we pull it off? No one knew. In fact, the goal might be utterly impossible. Yet Kennedy's vision had captured America's imagination.

The opportunity for great communicating was tremendous. JFK knew this; he understood and recognized the opportunity—and seized it. It wouldn't be enough to simply Direct efforts using his authority as president. To win the support of Americans for this BHAG, he *had* to map his destination to create an Inspire experience, and he had to recalculate his message each time. How could he shift the experience so that it connected with the audience at a university versus a health center? How would he modify his message each time so that his listeners would feel moved to act? How could he shift them from, "I was given orders. I have to," to, "Sign me up! I want to be part of this."

Kennedy delivered one of his greatest speeches ("We choose to go to the moon") at Rice University in Houston, Texas, on September 12, 1962. He had to connect and make it all about them, not him. He shifted upward on the Emotional Connection axis by appealing to the desire to beat the Soviet Union in the space race. He spoke to our best impulses as citizens of the United States. And he brilliantly moved all the way to the right on the Content axis to create an audience-centered message:

"Its hazards are hostile to us all. Its conquest deserves the best of all mankind, and its opportunity for peaceful cooperation may never come again. But why, some say, the moon? Why choose this as our goal? And they may well ask why climb the highest mountain? Why, 35 years ago, fly the Atlantic? Why does Rice play Texas?"

The Rice students in the crowed erupted. Now that's audience-centered. It turns out that Kennedy added the Rice football reference at the last minute, and jotted it down on his typed, prepared speech (see Figure 9-1).

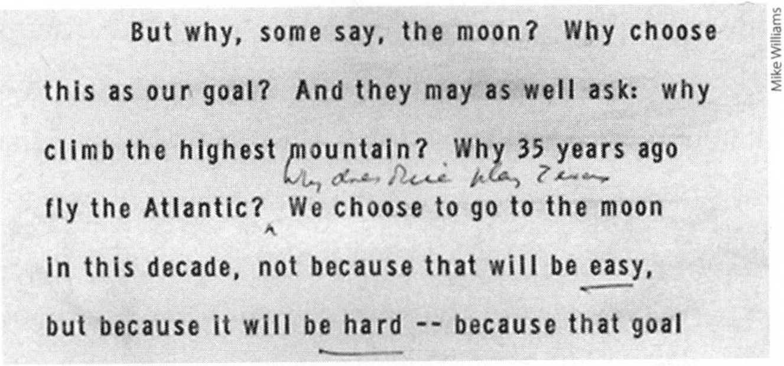

But why, some say, the moon? Why choose this as our goal? And they may as well ask: why climb the highest mountain? Why 35 years ago
*Why does Rice play Texas*
fly the Atlantic? We choose to go to the moon in this decade, not because that will be easy, but because it will be hard -- because that goal

Figure 9-1    Papers of John F. Kennedy. Presidential Papers. President's Office Files. Speech Files. Address at Rice University, Houston, Texas, 12 September 1962.

Looking back, on the fiftieth anniversary of the speech, Douglas Brinkley, a professor of history at Rice University, wrote:

> Kennedy's oration was front-page news around the country. . . . Kennedy made the case to taxpayers that NASA needed a $5.4 billion budget. Kennedy also did a tremendous job of connecting the moonshot to Houston in ways that thrilled locals. "We meet at a college noted for knowledge, in a city noted for progress, in a state noted for strength," he said. "And we stand in need of all three." What Kennedy did so brilliantly that day was frame the moonshot as being instrumental for U.S. security reasons.

Kennedy used communication to drive moon-shot efforts that would take place over the course of eight years. His message aligned the efforts of thousands of people across the private and public sectors to make the impossible possible. On July 20, 1969, at 4:18 p.m. Eastern time, the *Apollo 11* lunar landing module touched down on the desolate surface of the moon. Mission accomplished.

Even if time travel were possible, we know that you're probably not preparing to speak to an entire nation about going to the moon. Recognize the opportunities around you right now. Great communicating can motivate, mobilize, and have impact. You have the opportunity to change the way other people think, to shift their opinions, and to ignite their actions whether you're launching a new initiative for your colleagues, educating your customers, or planning a trip to the park with your kids (but only if they clean their rooms). Make them care, and you'll make a difference. Be concrete, and they'll remember you. Make them do something different, and they'll thank you. It all starts when you seize the opportunity to move from information to influence, and then take the leap to Inspire.

## PUT IN THE WORK

JFK's big communicating moments are firmly planted in the Inspire quadrant. He connected so naturally, and created such memorable and meaningful experiences, that you might think, *He must have been born with it.*

Amazingly, JFK was not *always* the charming, articulate leader of political lore. As John Barnes writes in *John F. Kennedy on Leadership*:

> A glance at one of his earliest appearances before a newsreel camera shows an awkward, self-conscious, almost impossibly young-looking man explaining his vague and inchoate plans to one day work for the government. "Charismatic" is not a word that would leap immediately to the viewer's mind.[2]

The gangly young Kennedy apparently lacked the eloquence and suave charm that later became his trademark.

How, then, did the notably *un*charismatic JFK become one of the great speakers of the twentieth century? Transformational leadership theorist Ronald E. Riggio explains that Kennedy *deliberately set out to acquire* the personal magnetism that he saw in the Hollywood stars of the 1930s. Riggio writes:

> As a young man, John Kennedy was intrigued by the concept of charisma, particularly the charisma possessed by motion-picture stars. Kennedy and a friend, Charles Spaulding, traveled to Hollywood to meet the future President's film idols.
>
> The two men made the rounds of Hollywood nightlife, rubbing elbows with Gary Cooper, Clark Gable, and other stars. . . . [Spaulding recalled]: "Charisma wasn't a catchword yet, but Jack was very interested in that binding magnetism these screen personalities had. What exactly was it? How did you go about acquiring it? Did it have an impact on your private life? How did you make it work for you? He wouldn't let the subject go."[3]

We don't recommend jumping on the next plane to Hollywood to find great communicating these days. We *do* recommend that you use what you've just learned. Like Kennedy, realize the importance of making a strong emotional connection. That, combined with Audience-Centered content, equals an experience where you Inspire. Now find examples of great communicating all around you. The ability to speak well, connect with people one-on-one, and inspire audiences is a learnable skill set, as you have seen throughout these pages. John F. Kennedy was committed to personal improvement. The same skills that made him a great and attractive leader are available to you. You just have to want them enough to commit yourself to continual growth and improvement.

## Natural-Born Communicators

There's no such thing as a natural-born communicator—which is actually great news for us! Sure, there are some people who may be predisposed to it. However, mastering the communication experiences you create isn't a matter of nature versus nurture. Rather, according to Carol Dweck, Stanford University psychologist and author of *Mindset*, it's the view you adopt for yourself—whether you have a fixed mindset or a growth mindset—that affects how you approach and react to pretty much everything, from receiving a bad grade on a test to getting passed over for a promotion and disciplining your kids.

If you have a fixed mindset, you believe that you are who you are, that there's a limit to what you can accomplish because that's just the way it is. This belief doesn't make you apathetic. Instead, Dweck says, it "creates a sense of urgency to prove yourself over and over." Your qualities are set in stone, so you'd better prove that what you've got is pretty darn good.

On the other hand, with a growth mindset, your core belief is that you can work hard to change; you have a passion for learning and growing. Dweck notes that growth-minded types think, "Why waste time proving over and over how great I am, when I could be getting even better?" You have that fantastic forward lean for continuous improvement that we love about great leaders. If you're reading this book, you're probably in the growth-minded camp.

Jim Collins found this to be a key element of success in the thriving companies he studied in *Good to Great.* The great companies were all led by what Collins called Level 5 leaders—those who "blend extreme personal humility with intense professional will."[4] Their growth mindset keeps them laser-focused on getting better—surrounding themselves with great people, testing approaches, and learning from mistakes.

If you have a fixed mindset (it's OK; many of us do because it was reinforced from an early age), the great news is that you can change. Dweck's research team showed significant improvement in the math grades of a group of junior high school students by teaching them growth-minded concepts like "your brain is a muscle that can be developed." With a small amount of training, these kids shifted from a fixed mindset that said, "I'm no good at math," to one that said, "I can do it"—and they did.

Regardless of whether you are growth-minded or have a fixed mindset, improving your communications takes work and a healthy dose of courage to get out of your comfort zone. When we first met Ernie Sadau, he was the COO and

THE 10X COMMUNICATOR | 231

had just been chosen as the next president and CEO of the CHRISTUS Health system, a $5 billion network of more than 40 Catholic hospitals and healthcare facilities in seven U.S. states and parts of Mexico. He was scheduled to take on his new duties within a few months, and he wanted to improve his communication skills. He was confident, engaging, and likable in person, but he felt he wasn't connecting with larger groups and audiences. He would stand behind the lectern and read his speech from a typewritten script, making almost no eye contact with the audience.

Ernie went through our executive training, and immediately embraced the principles of influence that we talk about in this book.

"Before my Decker training," Ernie told Ben, "I would write out my speeches in longhand, then give them to my assistant, who would transcribe them for me. Then I'd pretty much deliver the speech word for word. I wasn't terrible at it. I could make occasional eye contact with the audience; I could occasionally go off-script now and then. But I was not an exciting speaker. I delivered scripted speeches because, for 20 years or more, that was how I had seen all business leaders give speeches. It's the way it was always done, and I didn't know of any other way to do it. I just thought, 'Okay, this is what you're supposed to do.'

"But as I moved into the CEO role at CHRISTUS, I realized that the CEO is the mouthpiece for the system, so the ability to communicate well is the number one indicator of success for a CEO. I didn't want to continue doing what I had always done. I knew that communicating with audiences was one of my weaknesses, so I made up my mind to remedy that."

A few weeks later, Ernie took a huge leap of faith. As he was about to give his first big speech to the top leadership of the company—about 250 people—he was *briefly* tempted to hang on to the "security blanket" of a scripted speech. But Ernie was committed to making a clean break with his past ways.

When Ernie Sadau stepped onto the stage, he had no script—just a Decker Grid with sticky notes that allowed him to speak from the heart. Free of a typewritten script, he was able to make eye contact with his audience. He told stories and suggested an exciting vision for the future of CHRISTUS Health—and he was a hit! On that day, Ernie Sadau became a leader who inspired his audience to action.

While Ernie had the growth mindset that propelled his development, the coaching he received didn't turn him into something he wasn't. Instead, it gave him the tools, skills, and principles to become the authentic, effective, influential communicator he had always wanted to be. He discovered that he could make an emotional connection with the people in his audience, earn their trust, and convert their enthusiasm into action—and still be himself.

Ernie had the self-awareness to recognize that the experiences he created on the Communicator's Roadmap were not where he wanted to be or where he needed to be. He also had the courage to try a new approach. Through authenticity, he learned to Inspire.

## Authenticity: Your Natural Self

Our goal is not to create an army of communicators who gesture in the same manner, smile all the time, and project their voices. That's not influence; that's uniformity. Our goal, as with Ernie, is to make what's great about you come alive and stand out in every communication situation. A friend of ours told us a story about how she watched her husband present in front of a large audience at a conference. She couldn't believe what she saw—the man she knew to be light, witty, confident, and open when hanging out with friends and coaching their kids on the soccer field was suddenly so overly polished that he came across as robotic. She said, "What happened? It was like he had this out-of-body experience." In reality, he kind of did. He wasn't himself. He believed that if he was to be taken seriously, he had to be serious. He was polished, but he didn't show his natural excitement. Without that passion, he didn't connect.

Be yourself. As the great philosopher Theodor Seuss Geisel (yes, Dr. Seuss) said, "Today you are You, that is truer than true. There is no one alive who is Youer than You." Authenticity rules. Think about the person you are when you are relaxed and casual—at that backyard barbeque. Are you self-conscious about your smile? Do you worry that your gestures might be too big or your laughter too loud? Do you plan out every movement in advance? Do you make sure that everything you say to your friends is scripted in advance? Of course not. You are youer than you.

## Trust Authenticity

In May 2009, comedian Jay Leno passed the torch of NBC's *Tonight Show* to Conan O'Brien. After a strong start, the show's ratings went into free fall. In January 2010, NBC paid Conan $33 million to go away and put Leno back behind the *Tonight Show* desk. In 2014, NBC tapped another replacement for Jay Leno, *Saturday Night Live* and *Late Night* alum Jimmy Fallon. Many media critics predicted that Fallon, like Conan, was doomed to fail. Fallon's hipster style, they said, wouldn't play to the older *Tonight Show* demographic—and Fallon's *Late Night* core audience, they said, wouldn't follow Fallon to an earlier time slot.

What the media critics didn't count on was a special quality that Jimmy Fallon possesses, a quality called *trust*. Successful TV personalities are always people that viewers feel they can trust—from Walter Cronkite (dubbed "the most trusted man in America") to Oprah to Johnny Carson. Viewers will invite you into their homes if they trust you— and Jimmy Fallon comes across as sincere, authentic, and trustworthy. If being funny were all it takes to succeed on the *Tonight Show*, Conan O'Brien should have been a howling success—but whereas Conan's brand of funny comes across as sarcastic and sometimes mean-spirited (that is, not to be trusted), Fallon's comes across as humble, engaging, and authentic.

*Slate* media critic Willa Paskin observed that "Fallon's appeal is how earnest and energetic he is: the king of comedic kindness." She also noted the "authenticity" of Fallon's "ultimate-nice-guy persona."[5] And *Variety* TV columnist Brian Lowry wrote, "Fallon comes across as eager to please almost to a fault, and he treated his *Tonight Show* launch very much like a guy auditioning to be accepted into homes."[6]

Lowry meant that as a criticism, but he actually put his finger on the key to Fallon's success: Jimmy Fallon really *was* "auditioning to be accepted into homes"—and on the very same terms as Cronkite, Oprah, and Carson. He was auditioning for people's *trust*—and he used his nice-guy authenticity to win the crowd. He even opened his debut show by introducing himself and humbly asking for the trust of his audience. "If you guys let me stick around long enough," he said, "maybe I'll get the hang of it." He thanked his fans, talked about his wife and daughter, lovingly saluted his parents in the studio audience, and generally showed himself to be warm and relatable. In the process, he won the crowd.

Authenticity leads to trust, and trust wins the crowd. If you want to succeed, if you want to lead, then be authentic, be yourself, and be the best "you" that you can be.

Just be yourself. Sounds easy, right? Well, we know it's not because there are plenty of people (like our friend's husband) who don't. Maybe it will help to look at it from another perspective. Chip Conley, founder of Joie de Vivre Hospitality (JdV) and author of *Emotional Equations*, proposes another way to think about authenticity—as an equation from Figure 9-2.

$$\text{Authenticity} = \text{Self-awareness} \times \text{Courage}$$

Figure 9-2

We were lucky enough to have Chip speak at our company kickoff in 2014, and we asked him to address this very equation. But first he took a step back and told us a story about what inspired him to write his book in the first place: "On August 19, 2008, my heart stopped. Just minutes after my business presentation on stage, I passed out. Flat line . . . it was the ultimate wake-up call for me. The doctors could find no medical explanation for my heart failure."

Luckily, Chip fully recovered physically, but that experience, coupled with personal tragedies and business challenges, left him in an "emotional emergency." He began searching for answers. After much research and reading, he created a set of emotional equations to help him gain insight into his outlook, interactions, and relationships. This helped him begin to turn a corner, but not before he opened up to his leadership team.

The leaders of JdV, Chip remembers, "were living lives of quiet desperation," hugely affected by the Great Recession that had dragged down the entire hospitality industry, along with the rest of the economy. He recalled, "We were meeting at the Dream Inn in Santa Cruz. My entire team was there, and I was supposed to come in and deliver the rah-rah speech to take on the big challenges this year. But everything felt wrong about it. And even though I was worried about showing weakness, I decided to talk about my own vulnerability and worries, and I introduced my Meaning equation to the group. The response was incredible. There was this collective sigh of relief. It was like everyone could suddenly breathe again." The leaders felt connected like never before. From that point on, Chip began teaching Emotional Equations to employees at JdV.

In that moment (and probably unconsciously to him), Chip demonstrated the Authenticity equation. He was aware of his own struggles and search for meaning and was honest and courageous enough to share them. He said, "They're both vital. Self-awareness without courage means that you know who you are, but the rest of the world doesn't. Courage without self-awareness can lead to macho posturing. So this is a multiplication equation, because the alchemy of those emotions—not just their addition—creates authenticity."

How can you boost your self-awareness? You can gain a great deal from looking internally and doing some soul-searching. We won't cover that here (even though we were both psychology majors), so let's leverage the best resource outside of ourselves: feedback.

Kevin Durant is lucky. So are Tom Brady, Steve Nash, Venus Williams, Misty May Treanor, and Drew Brees. Not just because they're professional athletes, but also because they are constantly acquiring and responding to feedback. How can you continue to improve if you don't know where you stand?

There are three types of feedback that you can get (and give—start instituting a culture of feedback in your organization!):

## Feeback: The Path to Self-Awareness

1. *People feedback.* Use the 3 × 3 Rule. Identify three keepers and three improvements. What did you do well and should keep doing (those are keepers!)? What do you need to work on (improvements you need to make)? After every presentation, ask five people to provide feedback according to the 3 × 3 Rule.

2. *Video-record every presentation you give (a quick and simple way to do this is with any smartphone).* When you see and hear it played back, write down your observations according to the 3 × 3 Rule.

3. *Audio-record yourself at every opportunity.* When was the last time you listened to a voicemail of yourself? (In many cases, you can hit # to play it back and approve it before you send it.) Record conference calls and business/board presentations. You don't have to listen to the whole thing—10 to 30 seconds will give you a feel for the good, the bad, and the ugly.

Feedback can both build and erode confidence, depending on how it is given. We're looking to be our best authentic selves, not our most neurotic or downtrodden. So be sure that feedback is constructive. Also, make sure that it's balanced. It's our natural tendency to dwell on the negative. Be sure to identify as many improvements as you do negatives! We give feedback to clients all the time, and we also ask our team members to give us feedback regularly. Check out some of Ben's recent feedback in Figure 9-3.

Figure 9-3

And hey, if you have made it all the way through this book, you are demonstrating self-awareness. The question is, Do you have the courage to stop telling yourself the white lies and make a change?

# Humble Confidence:
# The Goldilocks Effect

There's something *amazingly* attractive about people who have found that perfect balance of humility combined with confidence. They skyrocket to the top of the Emotional Connection axis. They inspire and move us. Our response to them shifts from "I have to" to "I want to."

As a point of reference, close your eyes and picture Nelson Mandela. Is he smiling? Of course he is. You would never think of him as arrogant. He was strong and confident, but it was his warmth that propelled his success. He had energy in his voice and face and a lightness about him—even when discussing the heavy and serious topics of apartheid, brutality, and poverty. His humble confidence created influence and *inspired others to action*. From his first public speech to his last, he kept the focus of his message on others, rather than on his own individual achievements. Coupled with extraordinary timing and a persistent pursuit of justice, humble confidence enabled Mandela to take his place as a trusted leader not only in South Africa but also in the world.

The Behaviors of Trust show us how to project both warmth *and* competence. Too much warmth and you're a pushover. Too much competence and you're overconfident and dismissive. There's a sweet spot right in the middle, the place where Goldilocks would say, "Just right." It's the ability to appear confident without being arrogant, to be self-effacing while still projecting strength and competence. We call this special quality *humble confidence.*

Robert K. Greenleaf, an AT&T executive in the early twentieth century, coined the term *servant leadership* to describe this special quality of humble confidence. A humble-confident servant leader, Greenleaf said, "wants to serve, to serve *first* . . . to make sure that other people's highest priority needs are being served."[7] Centuries earlier, Lao-Tzu, in the *Tao Teh Ching*, wrote of the humble confidence of great leaders: "The highest type of ruler is one of whose existence the people are barely aware. . . . The Sage is self-effacing. . . . When his task is accomplished and things have been completed, all the people say, 'We ourselves have achieved it!'"[8]

Rather than me-me-me, a humble leader adjusts her Point of View to focus on *them.* Humble confidence empowers others rather than overshadowing them. It's not "my way or the highway"; it's collaborative. This urges others to step up and take the lead. A humble leader can step back and embrace the better ideas of others. At Google, this duality is framed as humility and ownership. "It's feeling the sense of responsibility, the sense of ownership, to step in. . . . Your end goal is, 'what can we do *together* to problem-solve,'" described Laszlo Bock, the person in charge of all hiring at Google. "I've contributed my piece, and then I step back."[9]

It's a big deal to our team at Decker, too. Lead with Humble Confidence is one of our core values, one that continuously reminds our team to move up the Axis of Emotional Connection. Here's how we talk about it:

> We know that we are the experts—the very best in communications training. But our confidence is special, because it's paired with humility. Humble confidence tosses ego out the window and serves others first. We shine the light on others, not ourselves. We take our trusted position seriously. We respect and honor where people come from, knowing that great communicators and Decker team members are made, not born. We all started somewhere and we share our personal vulnerability to motivate and inspire others.

Humble confidence, as a key to leadership and effective communication, isn't just a nice idea. Researchers Jeanine Prime and Elizabeth Salib of the Catalyst Research Center for Advancing Leader Effectiveness report that humility is the secret sauce in the recipe for great leaders and effective speakers. They offer some suggestions for demonstrating humility and warmth in our presentations, meetings, and one-on-one interactions:

- *Share your mistakes as teachable moments.* People who share their imperfections and foibles appear more "human," more like us.

- *Engage in dialogue, not debates.* Another way to practice humility is to truly engage with different points of view.

- *Embrace uncertainty.* When leaders humbly admit that they don't have all the answers, they create space for others to step forward and offer solutions.

- *Role model being a "follower."* Inclusive leaders empower others to lead.

Prime and Salib conclude, "A selfless leader should not be mistaken for a weak one. It takes tremendous courage to practice humility."[10]

## Changing Habits Means Continuous Improvement

We keep track of the leaders we have worked with, and we check in with them from time to time. We ask, "How is it going? Are the principles still working for you?" A typical response is, "Well, I haven't really had any big opportunities to present lately." And every time, it feels like a punch to the gut.

There is no such thing as private speaking! And while it's true that we may not have formal speaking opportunities going on all the time, all of us communicate *many* times a day, *every* day of the week. We are *always* communicating, and we can practice these principles every day. Even if we are just talking on the phone or in the hallway, we can be aware of *the communication experience* we are creating for our listeners.

What is the goal of practicing these principles? Simply this: to get a little bit better each day. Kim Collins, the Olympic track and field sprinter from Saint Kitts and Nevis, said,

"Strive for continuous improvement instead of perfection." So how can you continue to increase your influence, little by little?

Dr. Thomas Gordon, founder of Gordon Training International in Solana Beach, California, identified what he called "the Four Stages of Competence" in any skill. Just as we learned how to ride a bike or play the piano, these four stages also apply to our communication behaviors and habits:

> *Stage 1. Unconscious incompetence.* This is where most business communicators are. We've been telling ourselves the white lies about communication, and we have no idea just how incompetent we actually are (or what experience we are creating for our audience). We blissfully maintain the status quo because we don't know what we don't know.

> *Stage 2. Conscious incompetence.* Here's where we start to understand what's wrong. We recognize that our skills aren't sharp enough to get the results we want, and that we need to change our habits or acquire new skills in order to correct that gap between where we are and where we want to be. Often, this doesn't happen until some embarrassing mistake or setback forces us to recognize our limitations (in our training programs, that happens as soon as we hit "play" on a participant's video recording).

*Stage 3. Conscious competence.* We understand what type of experience we create, and we are mindful and deliberate about delivering it. At this stage, we are doing the right things (hooray!), but our actions don't feel spontaneous. They are still conscious steps that require focused intention, not natural habits.

*Stage 4. Unconscious competence.* This is the state of nirvana, where you don't even have to think about it. Thanks to all the practice and repetition, all your ineffective habits have been replaced with effective ones. It's second nature.

Every communicator's goal, of course, is to get to Stage 4, unconscious competence. As when driving a manual transmission without even thinking about shifting or stepping on the clutch, or when Buster Posey (we're SF Giants fans) throws off his catcher's mask to catch a foul ball, it's necessary to build muscle memory around communication skills. But before we can get there, to a place where we don't have to think about what we are doing, we must first understand where we are now as communicators.

Using the Communicator's Roadmap and being intentional about the experiences you create *can be transformational* if you let it. You might begin by working to become a better communicator, but soon you will discover that you're becoming a better leader in your organization, a better partner in your marriage, a better parent to your children, and a better friend to your friends.

But remember, it's not about you. You have a bigger call to answer. You must Inspire on a whole new level.

## ANSWER THE CALL

Ten months after Neil Armstrong set foot on the moon, Astro Teller was born in Cambridge, England. Though it has been decades since the last Apollo mission landed on the moon, Astro Teller carries on JFK's tradition of moon-shot thinking. Teller's official title is "Captain of Moonshots" for Google X, the secret innovation lab that has the task of tackling the seemingly impossible: self-driving cars; Internet balloons; wearable computers; glucose-measuring contact lenses. The moon shots at Google X are "just crazy enough" versions of a sci-fi movie.

Teller draws inspiration from that first moon shot, saying, "We chose to go to the moon, John F. Kennedy said, not because it was easy . . . but because it was hard. . . . Kennedy understood that the size of the challenge actually motivates people: that bigger challenges create passion."

Unfortunately, moon-shot thinking is in short supply today. Few of us dare to reach for BHAGs. Few of our organizations have the imagination and audacity to shoot for the moon. Instead, Teller says, most of us settle for trying to make something 10 percent better than it is. That's also true for most of us when we work on our communication skills. We think, "If I can get 10 percent better, that's noticeable. That's good enough. I'll get by." But moon-shot thinking tries to make things *10 times better*—that is, 1,000 percent better. That's why Teller refers to moon-shot thinking as "10X thinking." He explains:

> It's often easier to make something 10 times better than it is to make it 10 percent better. . . . Because when you're working to make things 10 percent better, you inevitably focus on the existing tools and assumptions. . . .
>
> But when you aim for a 10X gain, you lean instead on bravery and creativity—the kind that, literally and metaphorically, can put a man on the moon. . . .
>
> And that, counterintuitively, makes the hardest things much easier to accomplish than you might think.

What if you became a 10X communicator? What if you were able to ratchet up your connection enough to *inspire them* with a 10X gain? What could you accomplish? What type of influence could you wield every day?

Human problems, Teller adds, are "exponentiating"— growing and multiplying on an exponential curve. Traditional 10 percent thinking isn't up to the challenge of rapid change and the rapid proliferation of human problems. We need 10X thinking, and lots of it, to deal with the complex array of challenges that we face in the twenty-first century.

Moon-shot thinking doesn't always involve technology. Teller says that the Salt March of 1930 (Mohandas Gandhi's nonviolent tax protest against British rule in India) and the civil rights movement in America (exemplified in Dr. King's 10X "I Have a Dream" speech) were "social moon shots." Moon-shot thinking takes a massive problem, proposes a radical (and even improbable) solution, collects evidence that the radical solution might not be as insane as it seems, and proceeds to bring passion, imagination, and perseverance to bear on a solution.

Teller wants us to know that moon-shot thinking isn't just for an elite circle of eggheads in a secret laboratory in Mountain View, California. "All of us can come up with solutions for society's most intractable issues," he adds. "We can train ourselves to make moon-shot thinking not an occasional thing but a habit of mind."[11]

The problems facing our world today demand moon-shot thinking. But without great communicating—10X communicating—all that thinking might go to waste. Ideas cannot survive and thrive without great communicators to tell their stories.

The ability to communicate is the power to shift people's thinking. It's the power to influence and generate action on a massive scale. This is no time to think small. Now is the time to unleash the power within us, the power to communicate Big Ideas to the world around us. Become a 10X communicator who moves from information to influence, who builds trust, grabs attention, and delivers inspiration. You have the tools to begin.

The Communicator's Roadmap points the way. Plot your destination, then move up the axis of Emotional Connection and move right toward Audience-Centered content. Focus on *them*: your audience, whether it's one or one hundred. Stop telling yourself little lies and let go of the "security blanket" of your written script, your teleprompter, or your cheat screen. Connect through the Behaviors of Trust. Use the Decker Grid to go unscripted, and add a SHARP or two.

It's fine to use your communicating power to promote your products and services, to motivate your sales force, to ignite a love of learning in your students, to campaign for your values and attract voters to your cause, and more. You should use your communicating skills to achieve your personal, professional, and career goals.

But why stop there?

Why not use these skills and principles to raise millions for your favorite charity? Why not use your communication skills to raise awareness of abused, neglected, and exploited children? Or to rally your community to fight poverty? Or to inspire your fellow church members to get involved in foster parenting and adoption? People around you want to be part of something bigger—they're thirsting for inspiration and begging to be moved. It's time to answer the call.

As Kennedy said, we do these things not because they are easy, but because they are hard. The effort is worth it. If you put what you learned into practice, you will get there (Figure 9-4).

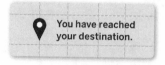

Figure 9-4

But the journey doesn't end. Our hope is that you will never stop seeking, pushing, and challenging yourself to communicate to influence. You will see opportunities with a whole new lens. Informing, Entertaining, or Directing is not enough. Inspire!

# Appendix

December 28, 2008

Transcript of the Caroline Kennedy Interview*

Following is a transcript of an interview with Caroline Kennedy conducted by Nicholas Confessore and David M. Halbfinger of the *New York Times*.

**DH:** Thank you for doing this.

**CK:** Thank you. (Laughs)

**DH:** Yeah, sure. I think we want to try and avoid questions you've already answered before and just get to the ones that would be somewhat newsworthy.

**NC:** Let's talk a little bit about some of the other candidates who are interested in this job. Andrew Cuomo: he's been attorney general, he's been a cabinet secretary, he's been a close adviser to a governor. He has an extensive record and knows upstate like the back of his hand. Tell me why the governor should pick you over Andrew Cuomo.

**CK:** I'm, you know, actually, Andrew Cuomo is someone I've known for many, many years and we've talked, you know, throughout this process, so, you know, we have a really good relationship and I admire the work

---

he's doing now and what he's done, so I'm not really going to kind of criticize any of these other candidates, because I think there are a lot of people with great experience, and, you know, any one of which the governor could easily pick and they'd do a good job.

**NC:** I'm not asking you to criticize; I'm saying, why should he pick you over any of these other ones, what makes you the best candidate?

**CK:** Well, it obviously depends what the governor is looking for. I can tell you what I think I'd bring to this, which is, you know, I'm not a conventional choice, I haven't followed the traditional path, but I do think I'd bring a kind of a lifetime of experience that is relevant to this job. I think that what we've seen over the last year, and particularly and even up to the last—is that there's a lot of different ways that people are coming to public life now, and it's not only the traditional path. Even in the New York delegation, you know, some of our great senators—Hillary Clinton, Pat Moynihan—came from, you know, other walks of life. We've got Carolyn McCarthy, John Hall, both of them have an unconventional background, so I don't think that that is, uh—so I think in many ways, you know, we want to have all kinds of different voices, you know, representing us, and I think what I bring to it is, you know, my experience as a mother, as a woman, as a lawyer, you know, I've been an education activist for the last six years here, and, you know, I've written seven books—two on the Constitution, two on American politics. So obviously, you know, we have different strengths and weaknesses. And I think I also bring kind of a lifetime commitment to public service, a knowledge of these issues, and I've spent a lot of time encouraging people, and younger people, to go into public service, through a lot of the, you know, nonprofit work I've done. So I think it's a whole, it's different, it's completely different, and it really is up to the governor to decide who would do the best job. But in terms of a family commitment—

**NC:** But do you think, in your own view, those things would make you a better pick for this job than other candidates?

**CK:** I think they would make me a really good pick for this job, and, um, it's up to the governor to decide, you know, who would be the best. Really. And I think there are many ways to serve, and I've loved what I've done so far, and I plan to continue, I think, you know, serving and advocating for the issues that I think are important. So, if it's this, that would be wonderful, because I really do think that the relationships that I have in Washington—you know, I worked hard on the Obama campaign, I have a good relationship with many of the people that are coming in to the administration, in the Senate, others, both sides of the aisle, you know, that's the kind of work that I've done outside of politics. It hasn't been sort of a partisan kind of career that I've had. So I think that at this point in time, that's what people are looking for.

**DH:** Do you think you would be the best for the job of the people who are out there?

**CK:** Well, I wouldn't be here if I didn't think I would be the best. (Laughter) Do you think you're the best for your job? I assume you do. Uh, yeah.

**DH:** OK. I just want to be clear, because you seem to be saying it's up to the governor to decide—

**CK:** Well, it is up to the governor to decide, and it is up to the governor to decide what's best for New York. You know, I think that I could advocate for New York, I think that we are losing a very visible, very strong, very powerful advocate in Hillary Clinton, and I think it's to New York's advantage to have somebody who can, you know, bring attention to New York, you know, bring four people from The New York Times here to the coffee shop (laughter) and really put that to work for average people. This is not, you know, about me, it's about what I can do to, you know, help New York get its fair share, help working families, travel the state, bring attention to what is going on up there. So that's why I think I would be good.

**DH:** Is it the path that you've been on that distinguishes you? Is it your skills and talents?

**CK:** Well, it's a combination that makes me who I am. Each one of us is a unique person. I may, and I think I represent a tradition that means a lot to me, which has really always been about fighting for others, for middle-class families, for working class—for working people, you know, and that's a tradition and a commitment that I take very seriously.

**NC:** Hillary Clinton was considered to be a very effective senator, obviously, even though she came in without much experience in a legislature. Is there any aspect of her performance, her representation, that you think you could improve on if you became a senator?

**CK:** Well, I think she spent a lot of time traveling around the state and really working to represent all the people of the state, and that's the kind of commitment I would make, so I think she did a great job, so I would love to continue in that tradition.

**NC:** You think you can improve on it somehow?

**CK:** Well once I—when I get in there, then I can really tell you exactly how I would improve on it. But as I said, I think she did a phenomenal job.

**DH:** Why is it that you apparently did not give Senator Clinton any kind of advance warning that you'd be coming out for Senator Obama?

**CK:** Um, I'm not going to talk about that particular process, but—

**DH:** Why's that?

**CK:** Because those conversations that I have had and had during that time are not something that I think is relevant right now.

**NC:** How come it isn't relevant? It kind of goes to your relationship with the person that you're trying to succeed in the Senate.

**CK:** I think this is about the future, and, um, you know, that's what I want to talk about, which is, what's going on in our state, you know, why I would be the best person to help deliver for New York. We're facing, you know, an economic crisis, the paper this morning said there's, you know, five billion dollars of construction projects which just stopped, you know, that's, you know—conversations a year ago, that's—beside that, I don't, as I said, I have conversations with a lot of people, and those are confidential.

**NC:** You said that you would run—and this earned you, I think, some applause from Democrats who were skeptical before, but you said you would support in 2010, whoever the governor appoints, but it occurred to me to wonder why: Why not run if you want this job? If you were sincere about this job, why not run in 2010 regardless of what happens in the next two months?

**CK:** Well, you know, I'm a Democrat, a loyal Democrat, I would support whoever the governor appoints, and as I said, I think there are many ways to serve and advance the issues that I care about, and I have a long time to do that, so I plan, in 2010, to support the Democrat.

**NC:** It just seems like the only—your interest in this seat coincided with the chance to become appointed to it, which is the easy way into the seat, and so it raises questions. If you really want it—

**CK:** Actually, I think that actually a campaign would be an easier way, because I think it would give me a chance to explain exactly what I'm doing, why I would want to do this, and, you know, and get people to know me better and to understand exactly what my plans would be, how hard I would work, you know, kind of . . .

**NC:** That's very interesting. Do you think it would be better for you, and for your purposes in public life, if the governor did appoint a quote-unquote "caretaker" and then just said, everybody can run, and that way you would sidestep a lot of these questions about the appointment, and whether it's appropriate to appoint someone who hasn't held elective office. Would you rather he did that? Like, if he appointed a caretaker—

**CK:** You know, this is all for the governor. And you guys are really focused on, kind of, the ins and outs and the comparisons of this process, and so, that's really something that you should be asking him. Really. Um, you know, if you want to talk about, sort of, the economy or the issues, or me, that's, you know—I'd be happy to do that. But—

**NC:** This is about your interest in the seat, though, and what drives you to do it, and what you bring to wanting to do it, so the question is: Do you want it enough to just run for it if you just had to run for it, if the appointment wasn't available, let's say—

**CK:** But this is where we are right now, so, you know, so I'm expressing my interest; many other people are as well. And I think that the reasons that I'm doing that is because I think it's a special moment in my life and in the life of this country, where there is this unique opportunity to help bring change to Washington. So I think it's a time when an unconventional choice is possible, more than maybe some other times, I think that I have a background and relationships that would allow me to deliver for New York. And, you know, I think that since this came up I thought about it really seriously, I've thought through a lot of these issues, of how this would appear and things like that, people always have opinions about, especially people in our family—what they're doing, why they're doing it, and I can't really think about it from somebody else's point of view.

**NC:** I understand what you're saying, but this is your point of view, because you're saying it would be easier if you ran for an election—

**CK:** I said in some ways it would be easier but this is where we are right now.

**NC:** So you'd rather do it with an appointment, you'd rather he not appoint a caretaker, this is the best way to do it for you.

**CK:** Um, no. I'm saying that this is the opportunity that's presenting itself right now, and I'm interested if the governor thinks that I could do a good job and help New York and help him. He is facing, you know, a massive deficit, he needs people, a team in Washington that can help, you know, get New York its fair share, whether it's transportation, whether it's the stimulus, whether it's TARP, and I think that I can be a member of that team and I think I have a lot of advantages to bring to that work. And I think the point of this all is that people are hurting across the state and in this city, and, you know, we have a once-in-a-lifetime opportunity to bring home a lot of the stimulus package, TARP funds, I mean, government is now poised to really invest in this economy, and I think we need to make sure it's done, right, and that's what I would like to do.

**DH:** We respect that, and I think we should talk about some issues, but I think we're really focused on how much you want it for the reason that, one of the big assets that whoever is appointed to this job must bring is the fire in the belly, or the stomach, or whatever, to run two times in two years. And so, we're just trying to establish how much you want this job. You've said you want it, you've said you think you'd be the best, but again, why would you say that you'd support whoever the governor chooses, and not run, in two years, if you're not chosen? It just sort of—we were thinking about the way that sounds, and it sounds like you only want it if it's handed to you.

**CK:** OK. Well, as I said, I'm interested in this opportunity, this is a complicated process, you know. I am a loyal Democrat, and I believe in the Democratic party, and I think that we need a team effort here to solve the problems that we have. So I will work with other Democrats, I will continue to advocate for the issues that I believe in, in two years, and I'm making that commitment, and after that, we'll see what happens. (Pause) That's a long time from now.

**NC:** Would you have sought this if there hadn't been an appointment open, if it had been an election?

**CK:** I think we covered that.

**NC:** What's the answer, then, if we covered it? Would you have considered going for this office if no appointment was available? If it was just an open seat in 2012? Would that have appealed to you?

**CK:** Well, it — 2012 is four years from now, and I just said that after 2010 I would think about, you know, anything, and I'm committed to these issues. This is the opportunity that's now. I didn't expect that it would come along, but, you know, a lot of life is seizing the moment and doing the unexpected thing. And I think, um, you know, that's an important part of life. So is working hard over a long period of time. And so, I am, as I said, I told the governor I was interested, he has a process, he has a lot of candidates to weigh, and he'll make the best decision for New York. And that's why I will support whoever he picks.

(Pause)

Is that it? You guys want to ask that again? (Laughter)

**DH:** Well, we did have another way of coming at it.

**CK:** Go ahead, let's ask that some more.

**DH:** Seriously, you know, everybody says, and the reporting that we did showed, that you were torn, that this decision took a lot of time to arrive at, at least a lot of thinking; your uncle, Senator Kennedy, obviously played a role in that. How disappointed would he have been if you'd have decided not to do it?

**CK:** Well, Teddy is—I don't think that's kind of, really, accurate in terms of the overall impression. But Teddy wants what would make me happy, and he wants that for everybody in our family, so, you know, he loves the Senate, he's spent his whole life there, and I think has been one of the great senators in history, so of course, that, that kind of an example is inspiring, but I don't think he would be disappointed in any way.

**NC:** I guess another way of thinking about it is that Jennifer Aniston movie, where she tells her boyfriend, 'I want you to want to do the dishes,' you know? And I wonder if Senator Kennedy wanted you to want to do it.

**DH:** "The Break-Up."

**CK:** (Laughter) I hope you're going to put this in the article, not just the answer. OK?

**DH:** I mean, was there anything wistful about it. Do you think he was hoping that you would really want to do it?

**CK:** No, as I said, I think Teddy wants everyone to do what is right for them. And I think he believes in public service, you know, of all kinds, and you know, in our family—you know, my aunt Eunice started the Special Olympics and I'd say she's had an impact worldwide on the intellectually disabled. And, I mean, there's many ways to serve, and elective office is one of them, and obviously it's part of our family tradition, but it's certainly not the only way. And I don't think that Teddy would think for a minute that this was, you know, the Senate or nothing. I mean—

**NC:** No, I'm not—

**DH:** No, no. Nobody's suggesting that. I mean, it just came up. You were thinking about it.

**NC:** It just seems like he—

**DH:** I just wonder if—he's not giving interviews about it, you're here, (laughter) and I think everybody would want to know: Did he get excited about the idea? Did you feel like he wanted you to do it? That's it.

**CK:** As I said, I mean, he loves the Senate, it's been, you know, the most, you know, rewarding life for him, you know, I'm sure he would love it to feel like somebody that he cared about had that same kind of opportunity, and I think he really—and so do I, think the impact he's had on, you know, working people, you know, the minimum wage fights that he's led, health care, I mean that's really—his example is something that, as I said, inspires me, because of the impact that he's been able to have. Whether it's voting, civil rights, you know, across the board, and I think he's shown that the Senate can have that kind of an impact on people's daily lives. And that's what's appealing about this opportunity, and I mean, I think, for those reasons he would love to have somebody that he cares about following, you know, that tradition. But I think in terms of me, you know, he doesn't care, you know, he's happy if I'm happy.

**NC:** Can you tell us a bit about, on a similar note, people are very, very curious about the days in which you were weighing this, and who you talked to about it, and whose thoughts influenced you and inspired you as you were weighing this in your mind. Can you tell us, who was the first person you had a serious discussions of, like, 'If I went for this, how would it work and what would it look like?' Who was the first person you really talked to about it?

**DH:** Where you took it seriously.

**NC:** Where it was live.

**CK:** Um, well, I obviously talked to my husband and my children, you know, the family, friends, uh—

**DH:** Outside of your immediately family. Can you say who the first person was?

**CK:** You know, I mean, also people started talking to me about it, so it was kind of a process, you know—

**DH:** Was there one, like, kind of, like—

**NC:** . . . tada moment?

**DH:** Yeah, where you actually kind of, in your own mind, started to say, 'Huh, that's like—maybe I really will think about this.'

**CK:** Well I think, as I said, there was, first—no, uh, you're, uh—somebody dropped off 200 signs at my husband's office, like, the day after all this was going on. So I felt with that—you know, so, and it builds. And, you know, I had conversations with Antonia Hernandez from the Mexican-American Legal Defense Fund in California, and I thought, well, she's someone I really respect, her legal mind, her sense of that community. And then there were people who I would run into during that period of time that, uh, people here in New York as well as people that I know from around the country, and I was up at the Institute of Politics meeting and I saw Elaine Chao, who's the Secretary of Labor now, I know Hilda Solis who's coming in, and a lot of people who I've, you know—Elaine Jones from the Legal Defense Fund, a lot of people that I talk to, you know, often in politics, and people that I met in the Obama campaign, who worked with me doing that kind of work. So I think it was kind of a broad range of people that, people that I'm close to. . .

**NC:** So when in your own mind did it go from, 'It's kind of an interesting idea' to 'Maybe I should do this?' (Pause) Or was that—

**CK:** Over the last couple weeks. (She chuckles.)

**NC:** Was there any moment where—

**CK:** No, I don't think there was a moment, I mean, this kind of thing is too important for it to be, like, an on-off switch, right? This is a process, and as I became more serious about it, and talked to more people, you know, I thought—and then obviously I called the governor and expressed interest, and um, you know, so . . .

**NC:** The signs were on what day? Was it before you called the governor?

**CK:** The what? Oh yeah, that was a while ago.

**NC:** That was a while ago?

**CK:** Yeah.

**NC:** So that was after Senator Clinton had announced—so it was after the vacancy became possible?

**CK:** Well, yeah. Obviously.

**NC:** OK. (CK laughs.) I just wanted to make sure of the chronology.

**DH:** We just don't know if it was after we started writing about you or—

**CK:** No, you guys had nothing to do with it. (Laughs.)

**DH:** No, we didn't mean that. The timing.

**NC:** Uh, so sometime before those stories about your discussion with the governor, sometime after Senator Clinton had been tapped for—

**CK:** Yeah—yeah.

**DH:** What was the best single reason not to do it?

**CK:** Well, you know, I think it's been a continuum, as I said, and I sort of first got involved in the city schools after 9/11, and I think that was really a defining moment for me, like a lot of people in New York. You know, thinking about, you know, how to become more involved on a civic level in this community. And I think over the last year, you know, during the Obama campaign, was really probably the most important thing that led me to this, because when I did travel much more extensively than I did in 2004, and um, you know, talked to people across the country and saw what was going on, and the impact that the campaign was having and the excitement that it generated, in both the primary and in the general election, and I think that that, uh, there's a chance to sort of bring all the sort of values that are, that I've grown up with and really turn them into something new. This is not about the past, this is really about the future and the moment that we're in, and I think that everybody right now has an obligation to think about what they can do to help. This is, you know— nobody can sit out this one any more. So I am volunteering to pitch in, if I'm, you know, if there's something I can contribute, and if there's someone else who can do a better job, the governor will pick them, and I'll work in whatever way I can in another capacity.

**DH:** No, but, my question was, as you were weighing the decision, what was the best argument not to go for it?

**NC:** A personal reason.

**CK:** Well obviously the arguments to go for it were better than the arguments not to.

**DH:** No, but I'm asking, what was the best—

**NC:** What was the single—

**DH:** What was the best argument against it? I mean, what was the thing you had to most overcome?

**CK:** Well I knew it would be a big change in my life, and I have really a wonderful life, and but, I feel like, you know, it's, you know, it's not really complete if there are things you could be doing that would benefit others and you're not taking, you know, the time and making the effort to do that. So, um, so I think it's really the, you know, it would be a big change, and change can be, you know, traumatic. It's different. It's good!

**NC:** How much of a concern were your kids and your family that you checked with them before embarking on this?

**CK:** That was a concern. You know, as I said, I think they are really politically engaged and kind of going through the campaign last year with them, you know, and with my uncle, and sort of having this kind of multigenerational effort brought us all closer together, and I think that's something that I think I saw in families across the country, where grandparents, people my age, and people voting for the first time all really felt that this was kind of a moment in time that re-energized people in terms of the change that needed to be possible. So I think in that way our family was like many, many others, and I feel lucky that I would even have, be considered for this kind of opportunity.

**NC:** Your husband hasn't been—wasn't very kind of visible on the campaign trail. I don't know if he traveled with you with Barack Obama. Do you think he'll be on the stump with you in New York, will he go to Watertown and to Syracuse and to—

**CK:** Well there's nobody who has a more supportive husband than I do, and he has a business that he runs, and it's his own business, so he has work to do, my kids have school to do, I mean, people have—there are other things in life besides politics. So he did come, you know, a few times, but he was home with our two children, home last year, so it's kind of a, it's a team effort.

**NC:** Do you think he'll be around the state with you a little more than he was last year?

**CK:** Well it depends on what's going on in his office. (Huffs.)

**DH:** I mean, does he have a desire to do it, if he can? Or, do you have a desire for him to do that with you?

**CK:** I mean, the more time I spend with him, the happier I am.

**DH:** Have the two of you figured out how to balance—I mean, among the other ways in which this is a change, is that it's a change, I assume, in how you each together balance work and family and all that other stuff. Have you figured out how you'll navigate that, if you become Senator? Or how that will change—

**CK:** Well since I've—I assume we'll navigate that the way we've always navigated everything. I mean, both of us have had a lot of commitments, you know, up till now I think we've both put our family first. And my kids are really supportive of this idea, I think they understand that it will make—you know, bring change for them. But you know, again, I think this is, you know, I think he's someone who's committed to, you know, education, science education, you know, he makes children's museums, you know, this is, he—

**DH:** He's had a really cool career.

**CK:** What? Yeah, so for him, that I would have this opportunity, I think he believes strongly that, you know, that I would be great, and that I, this is, you know, an unbelievable privilege that I have, and he's as concerned as I am about, you know, what we see here in this city and state that we both grew up in, and, you know, and that we both care about. So the idea that I can help people here I think is something that he totally is behind.

**NC:** Was he the first person you told—do you know if you uttered the words, 'I think I'm gonna go for this?' Or, something like it?

**CK:** Well, I don't know if I utter those kinds of words, but yes. You know, it was a mutual decision.

**NC:** Could you, for the sake of storytelling, could you tell us a little bit about that moment, like, where you were, what you said to him about your decision, how that played out?

**CK:** Have you guys ever thought about writing for, like, a woman's magazine or something? (Laughter)

**DH:** What do you have against women's magazines?

**CK:** Nothing at all, but I thought you were the crack political team here. As I said, it was kind of over a period of time, you know, obviously we talked about politics, we talked about what's going on, we've been watching the team that the president-elect is putting together—Hillary Clinton is going to be a spectacular part of that team, you know, then there was a vacancy here, you know, just like everybody else, you know: who's going to fill it, isn't that interesting, there's a lot of great candidates, you know, obviously I have become much more politically involved than I have in the past, so you know, I figure, why not try, I really think I have something to offer.

**NC:** But there was no one moment you can draw on—

**CK:** I know I wish there was, I'll think about it.

**NC:** If there isn't, that's what it was, that's fine too. We're not the crack political team, we're always looking for good anecdotes and good stories.

**CK:** I know, and I understand. I'll think about it a little more.

**DH:** It's not an executive branch thing, being a Senator, but there is a sizable staff that any senator manages. As you know from your uncle and many other senators, I'm sure. What management experience have you had? By the way, I think there's some curiosity about, just, what sort of staff do you manage now?

**CK:** Um, I, uh, you know, I think there's—obviously, you need to build a team, and that's how effective, how tough senators are effective. So I understand that that is part of the job. And I have been—but I also think it's the kind of leadership is also now, you know, kind of a public, there's a public role to it, and it's about building relationships, you know, in the institution, and in the other branches of government. So I think it's a multi-layered effort. I think that building a staff is something that I would have no trouble doing. I think the staff that we built down at the Department of Education in the office that I've been, first, CEO of, and now kind of the Fund for Public Schools staff, is absolutely outstanding, and I think I would be able to do the same kind of thing here. And I think the results there show that.

**DH:** Would you comment on just how, in your personal life, what kind of people do you employ? I think there's a lot of speculation about the Kennedy wealth, and the Caroline Kennedy wealth given that you're looking for this job. Also, I think it gets to the question of whether you can show that you are able to relate to, just, everyday New Yorkers. I think that's the vein that we're asking the question in. But, would you say how many people you have on staff?

**CK:** Well I've been writing books. So that, by its nature, is kind of a solitary occupation. And from time to time I have research help, but mostly I've done those completely on my own. So I am not bringing a large management—that is not my background, in management of large organizations. But I think it's much more focused on the individual. Most of the books that I've written have been focused on, sort of, the individual, and sort of, either a voice, a personal voice, or a kind of transforming event where they step forward to fight for something they value. So that's . . . and in terms of, so I don't have large staff—

**DH:** Do you have any?

**CK:** In my house, is that what you're asking me?

**DH:** Yeah. I think it gets to the whole, is there a Nannygate issue down the road.

**CK:** (Laughs) I think we're heading down to the—I have somebody who helps me in my house, and I have an assistant who helps me with you, know, kind of all the correspondence, I mean, I'm on the board of the Legal Defense Fund, the Commission on Presidential Debates, I have staff that I work with down at the Department of Education, at the Kennedy Library, so in that way, I'm managing, you know, staff in different places, and so that's really how I do that. They don't work directly for me, but they're people that I work with in all these different capabilities. So in that way it's kind of a decentralized operation.

**NC:** Have your personal finances been affected by the economic crash?

**CK:** Um, probably—yes. (Laughter)

**NC:** Can you give a sense of how badly?

**CK:** You know, I think everybody's—not as badly as a lot of people's, but obviously everybody's been hurt by this, and it doesn't matter where you live. And, I'm lucky that I'm not afraid of losing my home. And my husband still has a job. And that's not true for a lot of people. So I feel very fortunate, and that's exactly why I would like to help people who are in those circumstances.

**NC:** How much money do you live on each year?

**CK:** Um, you know, I'm not really going to answer those kinds of specific questions. If I'm chosen for this, I'm going to comply with every kind of disclosure that's available. If the governor has questions about my finances, I'm happy to talk to him.

**NC:** Is it $2 million? Is it less than $2 million? Is it more than $5 million? How much do you live on each year?

**CK:** Um, you know, as I said, if I'm selected, I'll probably be able to answer all those questions, but I'm not going to go into that right now.

**NC:** The reason I ask is because it goes to the question: What experiences do you have, other than the campaign appearances you made with the president-elect, that give you the ability to relate to how average people live, and the struggles they're facing now?

**CK:** Well, you know, I have grown up around politics, I have lived a very advantaged life, and I am very fortunate, and I think that—but our family tradition has been always to work for, as I said, for working people, and I think my experience in the New York City Public Schools, you know, I've been doing that for six years, and I have a real understanding of the kind of struggles that people are facing. Many of those families are headed by women who are poor, and the kids are poor. So I think that I've seen firsthand, and extensively across this city, the need that there is, the disadvantage those kids are at when they enter school without the kind of support that kids from more fortunate backgrounds have, and the long-term impact of that on our city. We have a dropout rate that is still way too high, these kids aren't graduating. So I've spent a lot of time throughout my life working in the community here, and in politics, so I think I'll have a pretty good understanding.

**NC:** How much of that job in the city schools involved going to schools? Did you do a lot of on-site stuff?

**CK:** I do a lot of on-site visits, you know, I think the job was really to connect these schools with the broader city communities, so that involved both working with the business community, training—to train, you know, set up the Leadership Academy to train new principals. So that involved going to meet with business leaders, it also involved many trips to meet the new principals and the schools that they would be working in. When it's an arts curriculum that we put together, we had the cultural community come in and work with the Department of Education, you know, that's trips to the schools where the arts education is being delivered or not delivered, and we did a census, basically, on what kind of arts were going on, how many kids are exposed to how many disciplines of art throughout the city, so that requires a lot of time, too.

**NC:** How many schools would you say you've visited over the course of that work?

**CK:** I can get you that number because they have a track of it, the Department of Education.

**NC:** There have been some discrepancies in the reporting on your job there, which grants you were involved in, like the Gates grant. Some people say that you brought that one in, or, I think Joel Klein said you brought that one in; some former employees of the fund said, actually that grant was pretty much already in the works. Do you feel like maybe the people who are fans of yours have been trying to bolster you perhaps a little too much, and maybe giving you too much credit for the fund-raising?

**CK:** Well, the Fund for Public Schools was started in the '80s, and it really functioned as a sort of a pass-through for specific school donations over a certain amount. And it brought in about an average of $2 million a year, with more after 9/11 that was mostly intended for the Lower Manhattan schools. So when we kind of relaunched it and revitalized it, you know, now we've raised $238 million since then. So I think that, whether it's the Leadership Academy, the Gates grant that you're speaking of, you know, went to many of the partner organizations who are developing, starting small high schools. But I think that, right at the end there, I played an important role. So I'm not claiming all the credit for the setup, for the planning—those are planning grants for 51 small high schools—I mean $51 million for small high schools. So this work had been going on for a long time. But there was still a pretty—a skepticism about private funds going to public education, how they were used, and whether there were results. And what we really focused on, what I really focused on, was trying to target those funds to initiatives that would have an impact across the whole system. Because there are a lot of organizations that either work in individual schools, do partnerships, do, you know, arts education services, many other kinds of CBOs and faith-based organizations that work across the system. But there isn't anybody else who's targeting the whole system, so that was kind of an issue we defined for ourselves, and I think that's why it's been effective.

**NC:** So your precise role in the Gates grant was what? You came in at the end . . .

**CK:** It coincided with the time that I came into the department, and I think it was important to Bill Gates that I was there.

**DH:** What do you mean? I don't get it. Just that you were there physically? Or just that you had arrived?

**CK:** Well I don't know, you gotta ask him. But I think I, um—

**DH:** Do you deserve the credit that people are giving you for having helped to bring it in?

**CK:** Some of the credit, yeah.

**DH:** Can you talk about—given your work for the city schools, your support for the schools, we have to ask, though there's nothing wrong with the choice, why you chose to send your own children to private school? What was it about, why exactly did you decide to keep them out of the public schools and go to the schools that they did?

**CK:** Well, they were already in school, and they were in middle school, I think, and in high school when I joined—yeah, so—

**DH:** When you started to work, yeah. But at the point that you decided to send them to private school, why? What was the reason?

**CK:** Why? Well, I think that I made a decision that was best for our family, and I think that everybody should have, obviously, excellent choices, and that's—I want every kid to have the same kind of opportunities that my kids have. So I didn't obviously want to move them for my own purposes, because they were on their path.

**NC:** So you never considered public school for them from the beginning?

**CK:** I think that, for us, for our family, the schools that we chose were probably the right ones.

**NC:** What about an issue that's very important in public schools, and you've been involved in: teacher tenure. Are you familiar with Michelle Rhee's proposal to trade tenure for more money, essentially. Do you think that New York City should have a system, for instance, where, or even nationally, we should have a system where teachers should have the chance to give up tenure in exchange for a lot more money? Is that a policy you would support?

**CK:** I think that the whole issue of teacher training, teacher support, teacher compensation, attracting and recruiting—I mean, there are so many people that are looking to become teachers, and for the very best reasons. But I think that what we see is that it's a really tough job, and that we don't support teachers, we don't support the good ones, in a way that so many leave before five years are up. So I think that we need to do an across-the-board work on the teaching profession.

**NC:** Is that a good idea, though, that one idea?

**CK:** Well I think it's important to raise these issues. I don't—that's a really controversial idea, and I don't think standing alone, you know—Washington, D.C., is a separate thing. I mean, New York City has a million—1.1 million kids, 90,000 teachers; Washington, D.C., is a really, really small system. So I don't think it is a one-size-fits-all. But I think it's a national priority to support teachers and do a better job of training and certifying—

**NC:** But really, this is a single important issue, I mean, it would be good to hear your stance on it. Do you think that can work? Do you think that—

**CK:** I think it has to be done, you know, collaboratively with the teachers and with the union. I think here the school-wide bonuses that we gave, here, that we've done with the union and the city—I mean, that is, I think, a good model. There've been—Arne Duncan, the new Secretary of Education, incoming, has worked with the union and I think that the reform efforts that they've made over time will yield benefits in terms of student achievements. So if you just pick out the most controversial one as a stand-alone thing, you know, I don't think that's really the way to go about this. I think if people can vote it'll be really interesting to see what happens. I think there's a lot of experimentation going on around the country that we should pay attention to. But here, I think these bonuses that are shared schoolwide give everyone in the leadership team incentive in the school to work together to raise the kids', you know, achievement, and I think that's going to be an interesting thing to see how that works. And the schools, you know, have almost all signed up for it.

**NC:** So you're not going to answer about teacher tenure?

**CK:** About that specific proposal?

**NC:** Yeah. That's a big one. That could become a national issue, that could become—

**CK:** Yeah, it could be, so I want to watch—I haven't talked to her about it, and I know what the concept is, and I think it's really interesting. As I said, I think my initial approach would be to work with, talk to everybody involved with that and see how that is going down. And I think there's a lot going on in Washington, D.C., that's going to play into that.

**NC:** Do you think test scores should be a part of tenure decisions? Does that make sense to you in as one aspect—

**CK:** You know, I think there's also a lot of problems with test scores, and so, you know, I think we need to give the schools the flexibility. There's too much reliance on these, you know, NAPE tests. But No Child Left Behind is going to come up, right, for reauthorization in the next couple of years and that is an area that I feel I would bring a lot, and that's an issue and a set of issues that, you know, were I lucky enough to be selected that we could discuss, you know, in more detail, but that's something, an area that I have a lot of thoughts about.

**DH:** Just to talk a little more about issues: a lot of your political positions seem pretty straight-up-the-middle, conventional for a Democrat.

**CK:** Does that surprise you?

**DH:** No. But I wonder, what are the biggest areas where you disagree with Democratic party orthodoxy? We want to know what sets you apart. You've cited a lot of examples and influences; what would be a subject that we would expect your position to be a real surprise on?

**CK:** Well, I think that there's a range of views in the Democratic party. And you know, I am a proud Democrat, those are the values, you know—middle class tax relief, helping working families, fixing the health care system—those are the national priorities right now. So those are the issues that I would expect—I mean, I am a Democrat, that is, you know—I am trying to become a Democratic senator, so I don't, um—I mean, there are issues along the way, that I'm sure that people have differences of opinion. There's controversies in all these areas.

**DH:** One where you have a clear-eyed idea about where you stand on something that is diff—

**CK:** That is different from who? Anybody?

**DH:** The party platform. I mean, pick some standard. Just something that would surprise—

**CK:** I support gay marriage, I support, you know, I've had problems with Nafta, I mean, I don't—if we're not comparing it to anybody specifically it's hard to say where I'm going to disagree.

**NC:** How about Governor Paterson?

**CK:** But I'm a traditional Democrat, so that's what I want to fight for, those are the values I want to fight for.

**NC:** Is there any issue on which you and Governor Paterson disagree that you can think of?

**CK:** Well, I think Governor Paterson has—I can tell you two of the areas where I think he's done great work. Which is, alternative energy—

**NC:** That wasn't the question. Is there anything on which you two disagree?

**CK:** No, I'm not going to talk about my disagreements with Governor—I think he's done a great job as a leadership, yeah, absolutely.

**DH:** Two powerful, respected people are allowed to differ.

**CK:** They are. They are.

**DH:** We just wonder where we'll find out that you differ.

**CK:** Well, you'll find out over time. You know, as issues come along.

**DH:** What about Mike Bloomberg? I mean, you worked in his administration.

**CK:** Yeah.

**DH:** He's not currently a registered Democrat, although he has been in the past, and some say, you walk like a duck, et cetera. But, where do you differ with him?

**CK:** Well, I think what people are really looking for is for people to work together, and so, and, you know, you can laugh at that, but it's something I take really seriously and I think that we need Republicans and Democrats, all Democrats, you know, people need to look at what we have in common and what we can get done here. I mean, health care's a perfect example, you know, all the stakeholders are at the table. Barack Obama and Hillary Clinton had different plans, but, you know, I think the goal now is to get quality affordable health care and there's many ways of going at it. And I think the point now is to find something that's going to work, that's going to reduce costs and get more people covered. So I think, you know, now is the time for people to come together and focus on compromise. I think that's one of the things I have learned from my uncle. I mean, he's worked with Republicans, Democrats, anybody who can get the job done.

**NC:** Do you plan to vote for the mayor in 2009?

**CK:** I plan to vote for the Democrat.

**DH:** What if he doesn't get on the Democratic line?

**CK:** I plan to vote for the Democrat.

**NC:** Last question and then we'll let you go. What's your favorite place to visit in New York State aside from New York City and Long Island?

**CK:** What's my favorite place to visit? Um, you know, there's lots of beautiful places in New York and I have friends, you know, I've been to the Catskills, I've been up to the Adirondacks. I like to go to historical sites. So I loved visiting the battlefield at Saratoga.

**NC:** I think we're done.

**DH:** I think so, yeah.

**NC:** Thank you very much for your time.

**CK:** Thank you.

**DH:** If I can just throw one more question out there—

**CK:** I think we're done.[1]

# Notes

## Chapter 1

1. Nishtha Kanal, "Yahoo! to Get a New Logo with the Same Old Flavour Next Month," *Tech2*, August 7, 2013, http://tech.firstpost.com/news-analysis/yahoo-to-get-a-new-logo-with-the-same-old-flavour-next-month-103645.html.
2. Bethany McLean, "Yahoo's Geek Goddess," *Vanity Fair*, January 2014, http://www.vanityfair.com/business/2014/01/marissa-mayer-yahoo-google.
3. Dave Smith, "Marissa Mayer Overslept for a Big Meeting with Ad Executives in France," *Business Insider*, June 23, 2014, http://www.businessinsider.com/marissa-mayer-cannes-lions-2014-6.
4. Laura Petrecca, tweet on her Twitter account (@LauraPetrecca), June 17, 2014.
5. Rory Carroll, "Michael Bay Walks Off CES Stage After Autocue Fails at Samsung TV Talk," *Guardian*, January 6, 2014, http://www.theguardian.com/film/2014/jan/07/michael-bay-walks-out-ces-samsung-presentation; CNN Staff, "Director Michael Bay Freezes Up at CES," CNN.com, January 7, 2014, http://www.cnn.com/2014/01/07/showbiz/michael-bay-ces-samsung/.
6. Maggie Haberman, "The Hidden Mitt Romney," *Politico*, July 24, 2012, http://www.politico.com/news/stories/0712/78878.html.
7. Bob Schieffer, *This Just In: What I Couldn't Tell You on TV* (New York: Putnam, 2003), p. 378.
8. PBS Frontline, "Kerry as a Youth," PBS.org, October 12, 2004, http://www.pbs.org/wgbh/pages/frontline/shows/choice2004/kerry/youth.html.
9. David Rohde, "John Kerry Will Not Be Denied," Reuters, November 21, 2013, http://blogs.reuters.com/david-rohde/2013/11/21/john-kerry-will-not-be-denied/.
10. Kathy Kerchner, "Obama Beats McCain—in Public Speaking," Master YourMessage.com, June 23, 2008, http://www.masteryourmessage.com/blog/?p=85.
11. Thomas A. Stewart, "The Highway of the Mind," *Harvard Business Review*, January 2004, http://hbr.org/2004/01/the-highway-of-the-mind/ar/1.

## Chapter 2

1. John Stewart, "Video: Jon Stewart Mocks General Shinseki 'Mad as Hell' Quote," *Politico*, May 20, 2014, http://www.politico.com/multimedia /video/2014/05/jon-stewart-mocks-general-shinseki-mad-as-hell-quote.html.

2. "Hudson Demands Shinseki's Resignation," *Salisbury Post*, May 27, 2014, cited on hudson.house.com, Congressman Richard Hudson's website, http://hudson.house.gov/in-the-news/hudson-demands-shinsekis -resignation/#.U7nQzbGmVmM.

3. Richard Edelman, *2013 Edelman Trust Barometer*. "Executive Summary" (New York: Edelman Berland, 2013), http://mba.americaeconomia .com/sites/mba.americaeconomia.com/files/121501475-executive -summary-2013-edelman-trust-barometer.pdf.

4. Forrester Research, "North American Technographics® Online Benchmark Survey (Part 1), Q2 2012 (US, Canada)," May 2012, http://www .forrester.com/North+American+Technographics+Online+Benchmark +Survey+Part+1+Q2+2012+US+Canada/-/E-SUS1351.

5. *2013 Edelman Trust Barometer*, p. 2; Jeffrey Sonnenfeld, "Putting Trust on Cruise Control at Carnival," *Huffington Post, The Blog*, February 19, 2013, http://www.huffingtonpost.com/jeffrey-sonnenfeld/putting-trust -cruise-control_b_2720837.html.

6. *Edelman Trust Barometer*, 2014, Executive Summary, p. 7.

7. Julie Moreland, "The Shift from Chief Executive to Chief Influencer," *Fast Company*, September 27, 2012, http://www.fastcompany .com/3001612/shift-chief-executive-chief-influencer.

8. *Edelman Trust Barometer*, 2014, Executive Summary, p. 6.

9. Craig Timberg and Jia Lynn Yang, "Jeff Bezos, The Post's Incoming Owner, Known for a Demanding Management Style at Amazon," *Washington Post*, August 7, 2013, http://www.washingtonpost.com/business/technology /2013/08/07/b5ce5ee8-ff96-11e2-9711-3708310f6f4d_story.html.

10. John Medina, *Brain Rules: 12 Principles for Thriving at Work, Home and School* (Seattle: Pear Press, 2014), p. 87.

11. Thomas H. Davenport and J. C. Beck, *The Attention Economy: Understanding the New Currency of Business* (Boston: Harvard Business School Press, 2001), p. 20.

12. Richard A. Lanham, *The Economics of Attention: Style and Substance in the Age of Information* (Chicago: University of Chicago Press, 2006), p. xi.

13. Nancy Gibbs, "Your Life Is Fully Mobile," *Time*, August 16, 2012, http://techland.time.com/2012/08/16/your-life-is-fully-mobile/.

14. "Mobile Mindset Study," Lookout Mobile Security, June 2012, https:// www.lookout.com/static/ee_images/lookout-mobile-mindset-2012.pdf.

15. Karsten Strauss, "Do Millennials Think Differently About Money and Career?" *Forbes*, September 17, 2013, http://www.forbes.com/sites

/karstenstrauss/2013/09/17/do-millennials-think-differently-about
-money-and-career/.

16. Daniel Pink, *Drive: The Surprising Truth About What Motivates Us* (New York: Riverhead, 2009), p. 133.

17. Anna Maria Tremonti, "TED Talks: 'Ideas Worth Spreading' or Over-simplified Info-Tainment?" *The Current*, CBC Radio, January 13, 2014, http://www.cbc.ca/thecurrent/episode/2014/01/13/ted-talks-ideas
-worth-spreading/.

### Chapter 3

1. Waldorf-Astoria Hotels and Conrad Hotels, "Danny Meyer: The Key to Ultimate Luxury," YouTube.com, May 18, 2012, embedded video transcribed by the authors, https://www.youtube.com/watch?v=E
eJozd0GP5A.

2. David D. Burstein, "Danny Meyer's Magic Touch: How to Create 4-Star Experiences and Lines Around the Block," *Fast Company*, January 13, 2012, http://www.fastcompany.com/1807783/danny-meyers-magic
-touch-how-create-4-star-experiences-and-lines-around-block.

3. William Drew, "Danny Meyer: Pearls of Wisdom," *Big Hospitality*, August 17, 2012, http://www.bighospitality.co.uk/Your-Business/Pearls-of
-Wisdom/Danny-Meyer-Pearls-of-Wisdom.

4. Burstein, "Danny Meyer's Magic Touch."

5. Drew, "Danny Meyer: Pearls of Wisdom."

6. Rachel Emma Silverman, "Interesting Fact: There's a Yawning Need for Boring Professors," *Wall Street Journal*, February 25, 2013, http://online
.wsj.com/news/articles/SB10001424127887323864304578316162117673132.

7. Helen A. S. Popkin, "Zuckerberg Sweats Facebook Questions at D8," MSNBC.com, June 3, 2010, http://www.nbcnews.com/id/37491233
/ns/technology_and_science-tech_and_gadgets/#.U8MIVbGmVmM.

8. Albert Costill, "5 Things You Should Know About Mark Zuckerberg (and What You Can Learn from Him)," *Search Engine Journal*, May 8, 2014, http://www.searchenginejournal.com/5-things-know-mark
-zuckerberg-can-learn/103917/.

9. Robert Scoble, "What Caused Mark Zuckerberg's Improvement in Public Speaking?" *Business Insider*, March 25, 2011, http://www.businessinsider
.com/mark-zuckerberg-improvement-public-speaking-2011-3.

10. Ryan Tate, "What Everyone Is Too Polite to Say About Steve Jobs," *Gawker.com*, October 7, 2011, http://gawker.com/5847344/what-everyone
-is-too-polite-to-say-about-steve-jobs.

11. Romain Moisescot, "Steve at Work," *AllAboutSteveJobs.com*, March 7, 2012, http://allaboutstevejobs.com/persona/steveatwork.php.

12. Walter Isaacson, *Steve Jobs* (New York: Simon & Schuster, 2011), p. 353.

13. Romain Moisescot, "Steve on Stage," *AllAboutSteveJobs.com*, March 7, 2012, http://allaboutstevejobs.com/persona/steveonstage.php.

14. FDCH E-Media, "Transcript: Illinois Senate Candidate Barack Obama," *Washington Post*, July 27, 2004, http://www.washingtonpost.com/wp-dyn/articles/A19751-2004Jul27.html.

15. CBS News, "Person Faints During Obama's Speech in North Carolina," YouTube.com, March 7, 2012, embedded video transcribed by the authors, https://www.youtube.com/watch?v=mmPJw2Wrp4w.

16. Patrick Gavin, "Press: One Word Describes Obama," *Politico*, October 4, 2012, http://www.politico.com/news/stories/1012/82023.html.

### Chapter 4

1. Lily Oei and Aaron Dobbs, "Bob Tuschman, Food Network," *Gothamist*, September 19, 2005, http://gothamist.com/2005/09/19/bob_tuschman_food_network.php#.

2. Joshua Lurie, "Interview: Food Network Star Judge Bob Tuschman," *Food GPS*, June 22, 2011, http://www.foodgps.com/qa-with-food-network-star-judge-bob-tuschman/.

3. Amy J. C. Cuddy, Matthew Kohut, and John Neffinger, "Connect, Then Lead," *Harvard Business Review*, July–August 2013 (reprint), pp. 4–5.

4. These insights came from two studies Mehrabian published in 1967, "Decoding of Inconsistent Communications" (*Journal of Personality and Social Psychology* 6(1), May 1967, pp. 109–114) and "Inference of Attitudes from Nonverbal Communication in Two Channels" (*Journal of Consulting Psychology* 31(3), June 1967, pp. 248–252).

5. Malcolm Gladwell, *Blink: The Power of Thinking Without Thinking* (New York: Little, Brown, 2005), pp. 43–44.

6. Sanja Kutnjak Ivković and Valerie P. Hans, "Jurors' Evaluations of Expert Testimony: Judging the Messenger and the Message," *Law and Social Inquiry* 28(2), Spring 2003, pp. 441–480, *passim*.

7. Ibid.

8. Bert Decker, *You've Got to Be Believed to Be Heard* (New York: St. Martin's, 1992), p. 108.

9. Sue Shellenbarger, "Just Look Me in the Eye Already," *Wall Street Journal*, May 28, 2013, http://online.wsj.com/news/articles/SB10001424127887324809804578511290822228174.

10. Ronald E. Riggio, "Cutting-Edge Leadership," *Psychology Today*, June 25, 2012, http://www.psychologytoday.com/blog/cutting-edge-leadership/201206/there-s-magic-in-your-smile.

11. Sue Shellenbarger, "Is This Really How You Talk?" *Wall Street Journal*,

April 23, 2013, http://online.wsj.com/news/articles/SB100014241278
873237356045784408510836748898.

12. Nicholas Confessore and David M. Halbfinger, "As Candidate, Kennedy Is Forceful but Elusive," *New York Times, December 28, 2008.*

13. Toby Harnden, "Caroline Kennedy Repeats 'You Know' 142 Times in Interview," *Telegraph* (London), December 29, 2008, http://www.telegraph .co.uk/news/worldnews/northamerica/usa/4015918/Caroline-Kennedy -repeats-you-know-142-times-in-interview.html.

14. ABC TV, Shark Tank website, ABC.GO.com, http://abc.go.com/shows /shark-tank.

15. John Lee Dumas, "Barbara Corcoran," *EntrepreneurOnFire Business Podcasts*, December 28, 2012, http://www.entrepreneuronfire.com/podcast /barbara-corcoran-interview-with-john-lee-dumas-of-entrepreneur-on -fire/.

### Chapter 5

1. Jill Bolte Taylor: "My Stroke of Insight," TED 2008, February 2008, embedded video transcribed by the authors, http://www.ted.com/talks/jill _bolte_taylor_s_powerful_stroke_of_insight#t-223072.

2. David Lubars, "BBDO: Nice Is the New Black," speech at Cannes Lions, France, June 19, 2014; video no longer available online.

3. Andrew Stanton, "The Clues to a Great Story," TED 2012, February 2012, embedded video transcribed by the authors, http://www.ted.com /talks/andrew_stanton_the_clues_to_a_great_story.

4. HLN, "Zimmerman Defense Begins with . . . a Joke," YouTube.com, June 24, 2013, embedded video transcribed by the authors, https://www .youtube.com/watch?v=ZiI5bVurSo0.

5. Brené Brown, *Daring Greatly: How the Courage to Be Vulnerable Transforms the Way We Live, Love, Parent, and Lead* (New York: Gotham, 2012), p. 45.

6. Sheryl Sandberg, "Sheryl Sandberg Addresses the Class of 2012," Harvard Business School, May 24, 2012, https://www.youtube.com /watch?v=2Db0_RafutM.

### Chapter 6

1. Andrew Stanton, "The Clues to a Great Story," TED 2012, February 2012, embedded video transcribed by the authors, http://www.ted.com /talks/andrew_stanton_the_clues_to_a_great_story.

2. Seth Godin, "Girl Scout Cookies," *Seth's Blog*, March 5, 2014, http:// sethgodin.typepad.com/seths_blog/2014/03/girl-scout-cookies.html.

### Chapter 7

1. Dianne Dukette and David Cornish, *The Essential 20: Twenty Components of an Excellent Health Care Team* (Pittsburgh, PA: RoseDog Books, 2009), pp. 72–73.

### Chapter 9

1. Jim Collins and Jerry I. Porras, *Built to Last: Successful Habits of Visionary Companies* (New York: HarperCollins, 1994), p. 94.
2. John A. Barnes, *John F. Kennedy on Leadership: The Lessons and Legacy of a President* (New York: AMACOM, 2005), p. 51.
3. Ronald E. Riggio, *The Charisma Quotient: What It Is, How to Get It, How to Use It* (New York: Dodd, Mead, 1987), p. 162.
4. Jim Collins, *Good to Great* (New York: HarperCollins, 2001).
5. Willa Paskin, "Jimmy Fallon Brings Earnest, Nice-Guy Vibe to His First *Tonight Show*," *Slate*, February 18, 2014, http://www.slate.com/blogs/browbeat/2014/02/18/jimmy_fallon_s_first_tonight_show_with_will_smith_and_u2_nice_earnest_pretty.html.
6. Brian Lowry, "TV Review: 'The Tonight Show Starring Jimmy Fallon,'" *Variety*, February 18, 2014, http://variety.com/2014/tv/reviews/tv-review-the-tonight-show-starring-jimmy-fallon-1201110005/.
7. Robert K. Greenleaf, *Servant Leadership: A Journey into the Nature of Legitimate Power and Greatness*, 25th Anniversary Edition (Mahwah, NJ: Paulist Press, 2002), p. 27.
8. Lao Tzu, *Tao Teh Ching*, trans. John C. H. Wu (Boston: Shambhala, 2006), p. 25.
9. Thomas L. Friedman, "How to Get a Job at Google," *New York Times*, February 22, 2014, http://www.nytimes.com/2014/02/23/opinion/sunday/friedman-how-to-get-a-job-at-google.html.
10. Jeanine Prime and Elizabeth Salib, "The Best Leaders Are Humble Leaders," *Harvard Business Review*, May 12, 2014, http://blogs.hbr.org/2014/05/the-best-leaders-are-humble-leaders/?utm_source=feedburner&utm_medium=f.
11. Astro Teller, "Google X Head on Moonshots: 10X Is Easier than 10 Percent," *Wired.com*, February 11, 2013, http://www.wired.com/2013/02/moonshots-matter-heres-how-to-make-them-happen/.

### Appendix

1. Nicholas Confessore and David M. Halbfinger, "As Candidate, Kennedy Is Forceful but Elusive," *New York Times, December 28, 2008.*

# Index

# About the Authors

### BEN DECKER

The leading business communications expert, Ben bridges the gap between executive leaders and their teams. As CEO of Decker Communications, Inc., Ben has worked with hundreds of leaders in Fortune 500 companies to strategize and implement communications solutions that are practical, direct, and attainable.

Renowned as a speaker's speaker, Ben regularly addresses large audiences on the importance of creating a communication experience, developing executive presence, and the communications of a leader. He has been featured at large conferences and kickoffs for companies such as Marriott, Robert Half International, Hewlett-Packard, Million Dollar Roundtable, CHRISTUS Health, and Exponent.

Ben also coaches C-level executives from major organizations, including Charles Schwab, McKesson, Cisco, Bacardi, U.S. Coast Guard, JPMorgan Chase, AT&T, and Kaiser Permanente, as well as start-ups and portfolio companies seeking to raise capital. Ben's prior experience and success in sales and sales management in the telecommunications and surgical industries validated the importance of communicating effectively, even in the briefest interactions.

Ben has been steeped in the Decker Method his entire life. Early in his "career," he remembers being videotaped prior to his junior high book reports. In hindsight, he can certainly see the value of it, but the jury is still out on whether or not he'll subject his own three boys to the same. Family time is his most important treasure, and he's always protecting the calendar to spend time with the boys. Ben holds a BS in psychology from California Polytechnic State University, San Luis Obispo.

## KELLY DECKER

A keynote speaker, messaging expert, and executive communication coach, Kelly Decker unlocks the potential in individuals—especially senior leaders. As president of Decker Communications, Inc., Kelly leads innovation efforts, most recently developing new programs for challenges like Telepresence, team selling, and sales storytelling.

In addition to serving as the mastermind behind Decker's program offerings, Kelly personally coaches executive leaders from Fortune 500 companies such as AT&T, Clorox, and United Health Group to increase their impact and lead by influence rather than by authority.

Kelly has been a featured speaker at conferences and events for companies including Clorox, Microsoft, Newmark Grubb Knight Frank, Pfizer, United Health Group, and Wells Fargo. She helps navigate communication challenges specifically related to female executives. She has also been featured in the *New York Times*, the *Wall Street Journal*, *Marketwatch*, and *MarieClaire*.

Every day, she leverages the skills and past experience that she gained in consulting with the Alexander Group and in corporate communications and sales management with AT&T. She holds an MBA from the Haas School of Business and a BS in psychology from California Polytechnic State University, San Luis Obispo.

Having grown up in a large Italian family, Kelly has worked hard to overcome the communications challenge of overgesturing. She's also a proud survivor of growing up with three brothers, and she uses her experience to raise her and Ben's three boys, Jackson, Joseph, and Christopher.